Come Unto These
Yellow Sands

Come Unto these Yellow Sands

W. M. von Heider

Eurythmy, Movement, Observation, and Classroom Experience

Rudolf Steiner College Press

Originally published in Great Britain by
The Steiner Schools Fellowship
ISBN 0-9509430-0-2

Cover art: Leszek Forczek

Revised edition published in 1998 by

Rudolf Steiner College Press
9200 Fair Oaks Boulevard
Fair Oaks, CA 95628

ISBN 0-945803-30-3

Contents

Note on Pronunciation   x

Acknowledgements   xi

Introduction   xii

Foreword by Eileen Hutchins   xiii

Chapter One

Preschool (Ages Four to Six)   1

    Adam he had Seven Sons . . . Folk Song   2

    Summer Verse . . . R. W. Emerson   2

    Snowdrops . . . A. Matheson   3

Suggestion for Lessons

    The Feather Bed   6

    Snow White and Rose Red   8

    Briar Rose   14

    When the Spiders' Webs are covered with Dew   19

    Winter is Here   20

    The North Wind   21

    The Good Gardener   22

    Midsummer's Day   22

    Walking in the Rain   23

Finger Plays   24

Nursery Rhymes   27

    Hush-a-bye Bairdie . . . Song   28

    Minnie and Winnie . . . Lord Tennyson   29

Verses for Beginning or Ending Eurythmy Lessons   30

Verses for I.A.O.   33

Chapter Two

Grades One and Two (Ages Six to Eight)   34

Eurythmy Lesson Grade One   34

    The Water of Life   38

    Jack and the Bean Stalk   41

Copper Rod Exercises   42

Eurythmy Lessons Grade Two   43

Poems and Songs

On the Earth I love to stand ... E. Baumann 46

Sun .. E. Hutchins 46

The Sun Says ... E. Hutchins 47

Sunny Bank ... Traditional Carol 47

Christmas ... P. Wehrle 48

An Old Spanish Carol ... translated by R. Sawyer 49

Verses for Spirals ... R. Gebert 51

Up and Down ... G. Macdonald 52

I see the Sun ... Anonymous 52

What the Leaves said ... Anonymous 53

Easter Song ... M. Bucknall 54

Waken Sleeping Butterfly ... Anonymous 55

Butterflies ... W. M. von Heider 55

Midsummer ... R. Gebert 56

Dummling's Song ... J. Marcus 57

Song of the Twelve Dancing Princesses ... W. M. von Heider 57

Stepping Stones ... Traditional 57

Jumping over Rods ... Anapest ... Traditional 58

My Mother said ... Anapest ... Traditional 58

The Wild Beast ... Anapest ... German Folk Song 58

Verse ... W. M. von Heider 59

The Adventurous Fellow ... P. Wehrle 59

Stories and Legends

The Cloud 61

The Legend of the Scabious 62

Cowslips 62

Ladysmock and Marsh Marigolds 63

Snowdrops 63

Daisies 64

The Poplar and the Holly 64

Moss 65

The Convolvulus 65

Ragweed ... Verses by W. Allingham 66

The Nightingale 67

How Robin got his Red Breast 68

The Easter Hare ... W. M. von Heider 68

Why the Spider has a Cross 69

The Glow Worm ... Verse by W. M. von Heider 70

The Turnip ... Russian Story 71

Plays

The Gifts ... Unknown 72

Candles . . . W. M. von Heider   73

The Winter King . . . E. Hutchins   75

Michaelmas Play . . . R. Gebert   79

Chapter Three

Grade Three (Ages Eight to Nine)   82

Michaelmas Lesson   85

The Dragon of Ireland   88

Verses

Mother Earth . . . E. Hutchins   90

Grace . . . Anonymous   90

Verses for Contraction and Expansion   91

Harvest Song . . . Unknown   92

Our Daily Bread . . . W. M. von Heider   92

Harvest . . . Traditional   94

Apple Howling Song . . . Old English   94

Blow, Wind, Blow . . . Traditional   94

Scare Crow . . . Traditional   95

My Maid Mary . . . Traditional   95

Charm for House and Garden . . . C. Harwood   95

Creation . . . Old English   95

God with All-Commanding Might . . . J. Milton   96

Christmas . . . W. M. von Heider   96

Breton Carol . . . Traditional   96

Welsh Folk Song   97

One Misty Moisty Morning . . . Traditional   97

Verse for Rod Exercise   97

Concentration Exercises   98

Chapter Four

Grade Four (Ages Nine to Ten)   102

Grammar   103

Riddles   105

Contraction and Expansion   106

Can Eurythmy Help Children to Spell?   107

Verses and Alliterations

Words of the High One . . . Old Norse   108

Voluspo . . . from the Poetic Edda   108

Forge me with Fire . . . Anonymous   109

Marwick's Song . . . W. Morris   110

The Blacksmiths . . . English 15th Century   110

Steadfast I'll Stand ... Dr. R. Steiner   111

Unstooping ... W. de la Mare   112

Earth Folk ... W. de la Mare   112

Legend

A Michael Legend from Normandy   113

Plays

Harvest Masque ... Elmfield School   114

Iduna and the Golden Apples ... E. Hutchins   115

Chapter Five

Grade Five (Ages Ten to Eleven)   126

Poems

Thus Spake Zarathustra ... Persian   128

From the Bhagavad Gita ... translated by E. Arnold   128

Look to this Day ... Sanscrit   129

Akhnaten's Hymn to Aton ... Ancient Egyptian   129

Winter ... Lord Tennyson   130

Christmas Rose ... W. M. von Heider   130

Song from Pippa Passes ... R. Browning   131

Easter Carol ... Old English   131

Hilariter ... Old English Carol   132

Play

Persephone ... R. Gebert   133

Chapter Six

Grade Six (Ages Eleven to Twelve)   139

Greek Rhythms   140

Poems

In May ... Anonymous   141

The Fugitives ... P. B. Shelley   141

Fairy Song ... W. Shakespeare   142

A Song about Myself ... J. Keats   142

Hie Away ... Sir W. Scott   143

War Song of the Saracens ... J. E. Flecker   143

Pandora's Song ... W. V. Moody   143

From Pandora ... J. W. von Goethe   144

Hercules ... E. Hutchins   144

From Hymn to the Earth ... S. T. Coleridge   144

From Andromeda ... C. Kingsley   145

The Craft of a Keeper of Sheep ... Greek   145

Written in March ... W. Wordsworth   145

Chanticleer ... W. Austin   146

Hymn to the Sun ... Saint Francis 146

The Ride-by-Nights ... W. de la Mare 147

All Hallow's Eve 148

Play

The Lord of Lorn ... E. Hutchins 148

Chapter Seven

Grades Seven and Eight (Ages Twelve to Fourteen) 156

Poems

The Name of Man ... Russian Legend 158

Two Eskimo Folk Songs 162

Three American Indian Verses 162

Hymn to the Pole Star ... Anonymous 163

Michaelmas ... W. M. von Heider 164

Verse for Michaelmas ... Angelus Silesius 164

Behold the Plant ... F. Rückhardt 164

Spanish Carol 165

Christmas Eve ... Carol 165

Lorelei ... Translated by A. Macmillan 166

The Ballad of Semmerwater ... Sir W. Watson 167

The Temptation of Saint Anthony ... French 168

The Common Cormorant or Shag ... Anonymous 169

Who ... Anonymous 170

Chapter Eight

Grades Nine to Twelve (Ages Fourteen to Eighteen) 171

Newcomers to Eurythmy 171

Eurythmy with Grades Nine to Twelve 172

Alliterations and Verses

From the Vision of Piers Plowman ... W. Langland 173

Christmas Carol ... 15th Century 174

Ragnarok ... Translated by E. Hutchins 174

Dame Death ... Medieval 181

Dame Life ... Medieval 181

Christmas ... Anonymous 182

Ave Maris Stella ... Medieval Carol 182

From Hymn of the Nativity ... R. Crashaw 182

From Isaiah IX Verses 2–6 183

Verse ... Dr. R. Steiner 184

Space ... Angelus Silesius 184

God is as small as I ... Angelus Silesius 184

From Nature ... J. W. von Goethe 184

To Sea, to Sea ... T. Lovell Beddoes   186

Merry Measure   187

Old Rhyme   187

Old Song   187

My Heart Leaps Up ... W. Wordsworth   188

Pack, Clouds, Away ... T. Heywood   188

The Spring ... T. Carew   189

Vernal Equinox ... Latin   190

From the Book of the Dead ... Egyptian   191

Sun ... Gaelic   191

Planets ... from Goethe's Faust   191

Eurythmy Forms   192

Play

Midsummer Eve ... E. Hutchins   196

Four Medieval Verses . . . from the Statues of Nuns   200

Appendix

Advice and Indications ... Nora von Baditz   201

Quotations from Dr. Steiner   206

English Eurythmy   208

About the Author   212

Random Tips for the Eurythmy Teacher   213

Cross Reference Index for Come Unto These Yellow Sands *and*

And Then Take Hands   215

Note on Pronunciation

Throughout the book the German pronunciation of the vowel sounds and diphthongs has been placed first, the usual English phonetic spelling second. The notation used for phonetic respelling of words is as follows:

A	E	I	O	U	AU	EI	EU	Ä	Ö
father	mate	mete	mote	boot	owl	mile	oil	there	her
ȧ	ā	ē	ō	o͞o	ow	ī	oi	ė	e̲

INTRODUCTION

This book has been written in response to requests for material and guidance by Eurythmists, class teachers, and students of Waldorf education. It is oriented toward Eurythmy and the place of Eurythmy in the school. Eurythmy is a new art of movement, inaugurated by Dr. Rudolf Steiner in 1912, and based on the laws of language and music. It is, like all arts, healing and enlivening and has links with all subjects in the curriculum. This book is mainly for those who are familiar with Eurythmy or are involved in Waldorf education. No explanation of the art of Eurythmy as such is included.

In Waldorf education all teaching is done in accordance with the age and development of the child. In Eurythmy also, certain exercises belong to certain stages of development. This book has been arranged so that the characteristics of the growing child are outlined, for instance, at the preschool age, the seventh year, the ninth year, the twelfth year, and so on. Suggestions are made for Eurythmy lessons to correspond with the child's needs. Among the poems, legends, and plays are some "homemade" ones written by teachers or by children with the help of their teacher. Each is written for a special purpose, more as a working sketch than as a finished piece.

More than ever before teachers are experiencing the need for activities that engage the whole being of the child. Although specific Eurythmy exercises, sounds, tones and the like should be done only by Eurythmists, it is hoped that this book will help all teachers find the right kind of movement for their classes.

The following remarks and selections are intended to stimulate and encourage Eurythmists and teachers to work together, to encourage and guide them gently to find and create their own teaching material. A story, play, poem, or exercise, however imperfect, will always hold sparks of enthusiasm and engender warmth if it has been created out of the work with the children. This warmth will not only do the teacher and the children a power of good but will enliven the work of the school as a whole.

These selections do not by any means bridge completely the needs of the school from the preschool to Grade 12. They are intended as stepping stones. The very nature of Eurythmy is such that "ideas" arise from it. Creative thoughts have their dwelling in the formative life forces; one does not have to struggle alone.

To be a Eurythmist in a school is a tremendous challenge. How can Eurythmy be taught and tended so that life may permeate the whole school? Joy and enthusiasm, even on a rainy day, will take us a long way, but the real strength of Eurythmy lies in the fact that it is a practical path toward spiritual activity.

W. M. von Heider

Acknowledgements

I would like to express my thanks to the following authors and publishers for allowing me to reprint from their works in the companion teaching anthologies *Come Unto These Yellow Sands* and *And Then Take Hands:*

The Literary Trustees of Walter de la Mare and the Society of Authors for their permission to publish *Unstooping, Earth Folk,* and *Ride-by-Nights.*

Uitgeverij vri Geetsteleven for extracts from *Anregungen für Eurythmie* by Nora von Baditz.

Hawthorn Properties (E.P. Dutton, Inc.) for "The Seeing Hand" from *The World I Live In* by Helen Keller.

The Frank Lloyd Wright Foundation for "Prelude" from *An Autobiography* by Frank Lloyd Wright.

The estate of Selma Lagerlof for *The Christmas Rose* and *The Holy Night.*

Harold Ober Associates Incorporated for *A Catching Song* by Eleanor Farjeon, copyright © 1951 by Gervase Farjeon.

My most grateful thanks go to my friends and colleagues and fellow teachers in many Waldorf Schools for their generosity in giving their plays and poems. A special thank you to Elke Worm Jacobs and to Elmfield School.

I am also much indebted to many students of Emerson College for their encouragement and practical assistance in typing, translating and editing. To Rex Raab for many helpful suggestions including the title of these books. Lastly to Fiona von Heider for the drawings and for her good counsel.

Certain poems in this collection have been handed on from one teacher to another and although every effort has been made to trace the authors, it has not always been possible. Also, should I have inadvertently included any copyright material for which permission has not been granted, I offer my sincere apologies for this discourtesy.

FOREWORD

Come Unto These Yellow Sands is more than a guide to teachers and Eurythmists. Molly von Heider describes in an imaginative and observant way the growth and development of children throughout their school life from their entry into the preschool to their last year in Grade 12.

For the early years, outlines of lessons are given in great detail. These are full of creative activity, stimulating not only Eurythmists but all who deal with young children. The themes of the poems, stories, and plays are in harmony with the changing seasons of the year, and the moods alternate from wonder and devotion to humor and gaiety, so that the religious feelings—of which children are in so much need today—never become too pious or gloomy.

The suggestions to teachers provide support for the subject matter of the main lessons. As well as traditional legends and poems by famous authors, there are many verses and exercises created by teachers out of the needs of the moment. These are given not as stereotyped patterns but as an encouragement to those dealing with children to create their own themes.

Helpful quotations are included both from Rudolf Steiner's works and from those of leading Eurythmists.

Molly von Heider makes us realize what new life Eurythmy can give to every subject, so that what is taught extends beyond "head knowledge" to a deep inner experience giving birth to actual capacities.

Eileen Hutchins
Elmfield School, Stourbridge

Age Four

Age Five

Chapter One

Preschool (Ages Four to Six)

What kind of stories should we tell little children in Eurythmy lessons?

When we look at the drawings of four-year-old children, we see flowers, people, houses, and wonderfully rhythmical "scribbles" all wrapped up in the sun and sky.

If we look at the drawings of five-year-old children, we see that the sky and the earth are separated from each other. The people no longer have hands like suns; the flowers no longer reach up to the heavens. The earth becomes a hillock at the bottom of the page. The sky becomes a line or an arc at the top of the page. There is suddenly a big gap between heaven and earth.

This is a sign that the children are ready for fairy tales, kings and queens, princes and princesses, witches and wizards, stepmothers and stepsisters, gnomes and elfin folk. True fairy tales tell of the world from which children have come, and of the world in which they will learn to live in order to find their true kingdom and their prince or princess. The creative, imaginative faculty awakens strongly in the child at this time.

Three- to four-year-old children love stories too. They need stories of another kind, not of princesses and dragons, or of dark forests and wishing wells. Four-year-olds live in a dreamlike way with their surroundings, but their little limbs are wide-awake and active. They are all will and movement. They seem to be aware of all that is going on around them.

"He doesn't miss a thing," one mother said in despair of her four-year-old son. "He's never still either except when he's asleep."

Children imitate their parents, grandparents, brothers, and sisters — everyone and everything. They absorb not only the good, but also the harmful influences around them.

Children learn by imitation, repetition, and movement. It is the world around them they want to imitate, the world in which they are learning to live. Eurythmy stories for this age group should be of putting on big boots; going splish, splash, splosh in puddles; running through the pitter-patter, pitter-patter of raindrops; making cakes in big brown bowls — sifting the flour and shaking the sugar, cracking the eggs and mixing in the milk; digging in the garden, pulling out weeds, and planting seeds; going with the mailman on his rounds, knocking rat-a-tat-tat on the doors, calling, "Is anyone at home?" and if there is no answer, walking round to the back door and calling again; going to a farm where the munching cows say "moo-moo"; going to sleep under big blue blankets and waking up with the lark and leaping out of bed. All the "everyday" things are special when you are three or four years old.

Our old English folk tales, rhymes, and singing games are an invaluable fund for movement lessons. "Here We Go Round the Mulberry Bush" has everything a four-year-old could possibly need. Finger games are of great importance too. Little fingers and thumbs must learn to do all the sounds in Eurythmy so that they become neat and nimble, quick and skilful.

Little children love to dance to music and dance they should, but in their own sweet way, without the interference of adults. Let the lessons be rhythmical, but let the children move according to their own rhythms. The time to teach the children to step to musical rhythms is when they are nearing the age of nine.*

There are many ways of forming Eurythmy lessons for the little ones. Our Eurythmy lessons always began with an old German folksong, "Adam He Had Seven Sons":

This song was given to me by Effie Grace Wilson in 1932. She said that Dr. Steiner had suggested it be done with certain soul gestures in Eurythmy lessons in the English nursery class.

With arms up, we walked around the room singing. The second time, we sang, "But they all went just like me," very slowly and sadly with our arms in the gesture of sorrow. The third time around we sang, "But they all ran just like me" quickly and cheerfully, and we ran quickly, our arms in the gesture of merriment. The fourth time around, we sang, "But they all stamped just like me," and we stamped in the gesture of greed. The fifth time around, we walked softly with the gesture of inwardness and then stood still with feet together and arms in reverence so that our pianist would sometimes close the piano because he thought we had all gone home—it had suddenly become so quiet in the nursery. This became a weekly joke.

Our opening verse varied according to the time of year. If we began with the summer verse by Emerson, "For Flowers That Bloom," two children would become a bird and bee and stand in the center of the circle.

Summer Verse
Ralph Waldo Emerson

For flowers that bloom about our feet
For tender grass so fresh and sweet.
For song of bird and hum of bee,
For all things fair we hear or see,
Father in heaven, we thank thee.

---

*See "Art in the Light of Mystery Wisdom," Lecture by R. Steiner, March 8, 1923, Stuttgart, Germany. Anthroposophic Press, New York City, and Rudolf Steiner Press, London.

If we began with the verse about the snowdrops, five or six little snowdrop bulbs with their roots tucked in would crouch in the middle of the garden between the sun and the frost. After the last verse, they would begin to grow one little leaf, and another little leaf, and then a longer leaf, and, at last, a snowdrop flower would blossom.

The Snowdrops
Annie Matheson

"Where are the snowdrops?" said the sun;
"Dead," said the frost,
"Buried and lost—
    Everyone!"

"A foolish answer," said the sun;
"They did not die;
    Asleep they lie—
    Everyone!"

"And I will wake them, I the sun,
    Into the light,
    All clad in white—
    Everyone!"

After the verse, the children would all hide behind the hedge, crouching down unseen. The helper in the middle would sing in a fifth,

"Where are you all?
Where are you all?
Where are you all?"

And the children behind the hedge would stretch up slowly, saying,

"Here we
    are.
Good morning, wide world."

The teacher would then say,

"Arms to sleep.
Legs to sleep.
Heads to sleep."

Then our story would begin, a fairy tale for the five-year-olds, or "everyday" things for the four-year-olds. Sometimes with the four-year-olds we had to mend someone's shoe before we could go for a walk.

Sometimes we fed the birds and played the game of "Hello, little perky bird." Or we blew like the north wind and swirled in a snowstorm, and then built a big barn for the robin to hide in with his head under his wing, poor thing! We've made snowballs and snowmen, sandcastles and rainbows. There is no end to the building and making we can do with consonants.

At the end of the lesson, we stood with our hands crossed in reverence, feet together, eyes shut, and we wished. Or we listened to the birds singing outside, and were quite still before saying goodbye.

Rudolf Steiner says the following about the conclusion of a Eurythmy class, which applies to all classes right through the school:

> When the child does Eurythmy, he comes into movement; and the spiritual which is in the limbs streams upwards on the path of the child's movements. We set the spiritual free when we give the child Eurythmy. (And it is the same with singing.) The spiritual with which the limbs are full to overflowing, is released. This is a real process that takes place in the child. We draw away the spiritual, we call it forth. And then, when the child stops doing the exercises, the spiritual that we have called forth is, so to speak, waiting to be used. . . . The spiritual is also waiting to be established, to be secured. We must meet this need.
>
> We have, you see, "spiritualized" the child. Through doing gymnastics, or Eurythmy, or singing, he has become a different being, he has in him much more of the spiritual than he had before. This spiritual element in him wants to be established, wants to remain with him; and it is for us to see that it is not diverted. There is a very simple way of doing this. After the lesson is finished, let the children remain quiet for a little. Give the whole class a rest, and make sure that during this time—it need only be a very few minutes—they are quiet and undisturbed. The older the children, the greater the need for this pause. We must never forget to provide for it; if we do, then on the following day we shall fail to find in the children what we need.*

Little children need consonants, many consonants, to aid the healthy building of their bodies. They need music too, as far as possible in the pentatonic scale, or within the range of the fifth. The rhythmical structure of the lesson should be the same each week, but the verses, pictures, and stories can change according to wind and weather, season and circumstance.

When we teach Eurythmy in the preschool, we are working in the sphere of the will, where the child is one with the world. We are continuing the work of the gods. The tools with which we work are imagination, rhythm, repetition, and the child's ability to imitate.

Rudolf Steiner says, "In the third and fourth year infinite results could be achieved by the permeation of the child's body with an elementary Eurythmy."**

This is explained further:

---

*From Lecture 4, *Supplementary Educational Course,* Stuttgart 1921. Translation issued by College of Teachers, Michael Hall, Forest Row.

**Practical Advice to Teachers,* Lecture 1, Rudolf Steiner Press, 2d Edition, London 1976.

Let us think of the child, the incomplete human being, who has not yet attained to his full manhood. How shall we help the gods, so that the physical form of the child shall be rightly furthered in its development? What shall we bring to the child in the way of movement? We must teach him Eurythmy, for this is a continuation of divine movement, of the divine creation of man.

And when illness of some kind or another overtakes the human being, then the forms corresponding to his divine archetype receive injury; here, in the physical world, they become different. What shall we do then? We must go back to those divine movements; we must help the sick human being to make those movements for himself. This will work upon him in such a way that the harm his bodily form may have received will be remedied.*

---

*Lecture 1, *"Eurythmy as Visible Speech,"* Anthroposophic Press, New York 1931.

Eurythmy Lessons During Advent, Ages Five to Six

The Feather Bed

Long, long ago old shepherds stood shivering in the cold dark nights of winter while they watched over their sheep.

They would stamp their feet saying, "(My) feet are cold, (my) feet are cold."

They would smack their knees saying, "(My) knees are cold, (my) knees are cold."

They would even box their own ears saying, "(My) ears are cold, (my) ears are cold."

The shepherds used to stamp and clap around the fire singing:

> "U, U, U, (oo)
> I'm cold right through.
> What shall I do?
> What shall I do?

Now, there was a young shepherd lad who used to watch the old shepherds shivering. He would skip around singing:

> "When I am old,
> I'll never be cold—
> I'll make me a feather bed."

So he began picking up feathers and he would say:

> "Here's a feather,
> There's some fluff—
> Here's a feather,
> There's some fluff,"

and when he was as old as you are, he had a tiny bag of feathers, a bit bigger than a bumble bee. But when he was as old as the children in Grade 4, he had enough feathers to fill a basket. When he was as old as the children in Grade 11, he had a big bag full of feathers. When he was as old as your fathers are, he had a big

During Advent the "leader" can become an angel and wear a golden circlet and carry a little golden star-stick. Mother Mary can wear a blue headscarf secured by a golden band. Father Joseph can wear a brown hood.

The children can enter singing "The First Nowell." During the chorus, the angel can stand in the center of the circle, holding the star on high while the children do all the sounds in Eurythmy:
"Nowell, Nowell, Nowell, Nowell, Born is the King of Israel." (LLLLBL). Then they close their wings in E(ā) (reverence) and follow the star around the circle for the next verse: "They looked up and saw a star," etc., leaving out verse 3. Continue with verse 4.

Thumbs, chins, fingers, and backs can all be warmed up with anapests.

bulging bolster full of fluff and feathers, and when he was old, as old as your grandfathers, he had a bag as big as a bed—soft and full of feathers and fluff.

All his long life he had collected feathers and fluff, and now it was the darkest night, the coldest night, the quietest night the world had ever known; he was leading his sheep to shelter in a cave cut out of the rocks, and he said to himself as he walked along:

"Now I'm old
I'll never be cold—
I've got me a feather bed."

When he came to his cave, he saw a light gleaming. He grew angry:

"Go away
Get you gone.
This cave is mine,
And mine alone!"

He stamped and shouted and clapped. No robbers came forth, so he moved to the mouth of the cave. He saw a mother and a new-born babe. There was no warm bed for the babe. It lay there so cold and lonely. Then the old shepherd took his feather bed and laid it gently over the babe.

Then the shepherd's eyes were opened and he saw the cave was full of angels, full of light.

Mother Mary said to him, "Every year when winter comes, soft feathers shall fall upon the earth and all men shall remember the gift you gave at the Christ-child's birth."

Then all the children stand quietly, feet together, and have a Christmas wish before saying goodbye and dancing away like the shepherd did, full of joy to tell the other shepherds. (This story can be made to last through the whole of Advent. Always repeat part of the previous lesson before continuing with the story.)

Eurythmy Lessons During Springtime, Ages Five to Six

The lesson could begin with:
"Adam He Has Seven Sons" and a Spring Verse then lead into
the spiral with the words: "Off we go to the magic wood. . . ."

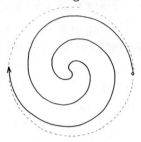

Holding hands, spiral in and spiral out. Then everyone will have their backs to the center and will have to dare to go through the magic wood again, in order to be the right way round.

Snow White and Rose Red

Once upon a time beyond the magic wood, a little house stood. Two rose trees grew by the door—a white rose tree and a red rose tree.
    In the house lived the mother and two children.

standing

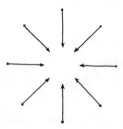

    Rose Red loved to run and race the streams and the rushing rivers.
    She loved to leap and try to fly like the larks and swallows. She loved to gather flowers.
    Here a flower, there a flower, here a lily, there a daisy, and so on.
    Snow White worked quietly inside sweeping and washing, washing and sweeping, making the beds, shaking the blankets, polishing and shining and shining and polishing the silver.
    Sometimes Rose Red and Snow White went into the forest to gather wood for the fire and then they would sing:

        "Off we go, to the woods,
           Hand in hand,
           Through the land. (*repeat*)

R
round circle

L

uu—
contract
W
B
Sh

uu—

Whatever we have,
We'll share together,   **skip**
And we'll never be parted
No, not ever."
Softly, softly, Snow White walks,   **slow walking**
We cannot hear a sound.
Rose Red skips and hops and runs
So merrily round and round,   **skipping**
So merrily round and round.

They watch rabbits hop, hoppity hop, birdies fly,   ʊʊ—P
fly away, fly away, Tom Tit sitting on a tree stump,   ʊʊ—L
darting deer, and red squirrels running.   **T, D**

I'm so tired, let us rest awhile. While they sleep,
stars and guardian angels keep them safe from harm.

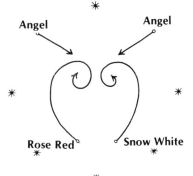

circle of stars and two
angels
Ah   Eh
Eh   Ah

The sun rose and they ran, and they ran and they   Oh
ran and they ran, until they reached home.   ʊʊ—

                                                                         **The children stand quietly
                                                                         and say goodbye**

(*Next lesson.*)

Every day in summer Rose Red picked a red rose, Snow
White picked a white rose, and they brought them to
their mother.

Here's a red rose for you; here's a white rose for
you.

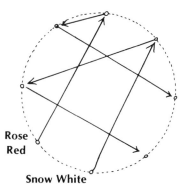

**The children never ques-
tion the two mothers turning into Rose Red and
Snow White. They identify
themselves with two chil-
dren and move across cir-
cle to two other children
doing U(ōō) as they go.
These two move on to two
others, and so on.**

When winter came with ice and snow, and snow and ice, and cold, cruel, cutting winds blustered and blew, mother made up the fire to warm the room. She put her spectacles on her nose and lifted down a beautiful big book and began to read. Snow White and Rose Red sat a-spinning while the whirring wheel rolled round, and the whirring wheel rolled round, and the little lamb lay low and the dove cooed, "Coo pee-coo, coo, pee-coo" on his perch with his head under his wing.

> When summer goes
> The warm fire glows,
> Close the door
> Keep out the snows.

A big black bear came bungling along, bungling along, bungling along. A big black bear came a-bungling along, brum, brum, brum, and he knocked at the door: knock, knock, knock, "Is anyone at home?"

B with arms and legs

Rose Red opened the door, then she ran and she ran, and she ran and crouched down to hide beneath the table, and Snow White ran and she ran and crouched down to hide beneath the table.

And the little lamb ran and he ran, and he ran and crouched down to hide beneath the table. And the dove fluttered and flew and fluttered and flew, looking for shelter.

But mother said, "Come back, come back. The bear will not harm you. Fetch the broom and brush away the snowflakes from his fur."

The children played with the bear and when they rode on his back and rolled him roughly around, he growled, "Snow White, Rose Red, do not strike your suitor dead."

Mother said, "Go to sleep by the fire, not too near, not too near, or your fur will singe and scorch."

(Next lesson.)

In the morning the bear said, "Let me out, Snow White, I'll come back tonight."

When the snow melted the bear said, "Open the door, Snow White, I must go and guard my treasures."

As he squeezed through the door, he caught his skin on a hook and cut it. Gold glittered and glistened under his rough fur.

The children went gathering sticks, singing,

> "One, two, buckle my shoe,
> Three, four, knock at the door,
> Five, six, pick up sticks."

"Here's a stick, there's a stick." Then they heard a cry, "Help, help, help!" and they ran and they ran and they ran. A dwarf had his long beard stuck in a crack of a log.

Snow White took her scissors and went snip, snip, snap, *(repeat)* and the dwarf was free. Did he say "Thank you, Snow White"? No. He said, "Silly Geese, silly geese," and scuttled away.

The children picked up their bundles of sticks and carried them home to their mother.

(The episode with fish can be done in a similar way.)

(Next lesson.)

Today mother said to Snow White and Rose Red, "Here's a basket for you, and another for you."

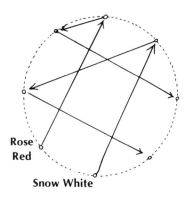

Snow White and Rose Red said,

"We will buy you some needles,
We will buy you some thread,
We will buy you white laces
And ribbons of red."

Off they went to buy needles and thread. On the way home from market they saw an eagle swirling and whirling lower and lower; they saw him catch the dwarf.

Rose Red and Snow White pulled and they pulled and they pulled and pulled the dwarf away from the eagle.

Did he say, "Thank you"? No. He said, "Clumsy girls, awkward girls," and scuttled away. They caught a glimpse of precious stones shimmering and shining.

The children ran home to mother and said,

"We have bought you some needles,
We have bought you some thread,
We have bought you white laces
And ribbons of red."

(*Next lesson.*)

Today Rose Red and Snow White went out into the forest, and behind a big rock they saw the wicked dwarf counting shimmering, shining jewels:

"One, two, three—these all belong to me,
Four, five, six—stones and sunlight mix,
Seven, eight, nine—all this treasure's mine.
Go away, gaping girls."

Big black bear came lumbering by. Snow White and Rose Red ran away, ran away.

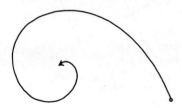

"Come Snow White, come Rose Red. Now the wicked dwarf is dead. There is nothing more to fear,

My brother and I are free.

They danced in and out of the forest trees. Then came the wedding dance with the princes and Snow White and Rose Red in the middle.

Round to the right, the right, the right,
Round to the left, the left, the left.
Up to the middle, the middle, the middle,
And back we go again.
And round yourselves, round yourselves,
And all take hands, and all bow down.

And so they lived happily ever after.

Eurythmy Lessons During Summer

Briar Rose

Long, long ago there lived a king and a queen. They had everything in the world they wanted except one thing—what could that be? Never a babe, never a prince or a princess, had been born to them.

One day the queen was walking slowly and sadly in the garden. She did not see the lovely lilies, or the red, red roses, or the tall tulips, or the deep pink poppies. When the big brown bumblebees and the beautiful yellow butterflies and the birds flew around her, she only said, "Begone, begone, my grief is so great, I must go and weep by the pool." So the queen wandered slowly and sadly along the winding path to the pool.

All at once—plop, plop, plop—out hopped a little green frog, and he hopped and he hopped and he hopped right up to the queen and said softly, so softly, "Be quite still and listen. A bonny babe will be born, will be born, will be born, a bonny babe will be born and her name shall be Briar Rose."

The queen was filled with joy, and she ran and she ran and she ran along the winding paths until she came to the castle. She called to the king and they danced for joy. Around them stood the lords and ladies clapping their hands, and then the lords and ladies took hands and danced around their king and queen. And all the world was glad. Then the king and queen and the lords and ladies and the frog put their hands and feet together and stood quite still while they wished a mighty wish for the little Princess Briar Rose.

(*Next lesson.*)

The queen she was a-weeping,
A-weeping, a-weeping,
The queen she was a-weeping,
A-weeping by the pool.

When out there hopped a little frog,
A little frog, a little frog,

The children will live deeply in this mood, and even the noisiest will probably try hard to walk slowly without making a sound.
   Squirrels, rabbits, hedgehogs, and mice might also want to speak to the queen.

uu—
It is quite possible at this point that the room will be filled with laughing, hopping, happy frogs that have no intention of forming a circle and standing still. The word "listen" with a Eurythmy S often does the trick: "Listen, did you hear what the frog said to the queen?" At least one child will know the story and tell of the baby that will be born.

The queen could tell the birds, butterflies, bees, poppies, tulips, roses, and lilies about the coming of Briar Rose.

In the next lesson repeat the story in verse form. A king, a queen, and a frog could be chosen. The king and queen could wear golden crowns and the frog a green scarf.

When out there hopped a little frog,
And softly said to her:
A beauteous baby will be born,
Will be born, will be born,
A beauteous baby will be born,
And her name shall be Briar Rose.

Then continue telling the story.

What is happening at the castle?
There is work for you and work for me.
What must we do to make ready for the coming of Briar Rose?
She must have a cradle, a rocking cradle.
The men will carve a cradle, a rocking cradle, for Briar Rose.
We will shoulder our axes and saws,

uu —

We will march with the men to the wood.
We will help them to fell a great tree for the cradle,
The cradle of little Briar Rose.

The master woodcutter asked the tallest and stateliest tree in the forest, "Will you be a cradle for Briar Rose?" The tall, tall, stately tree bent its branches low, and all the leaves rustled and said, "Yes, yes, yes, please let me be the tree to be turned into the princess's cradle." So the woodcutters cut the tall, tall, stately tree with a

"Crash!" can be done many times. K the crack, R the falling branches, Sh the flailing as the branches hit the ground.

chip, chip, chop, chip, chip, chop, crick, crack, crash!

Then the woodcutters took their two-handled saws, one each side of the fallen tree. And they sawed and they sawed and they sawed, very carefully, because it was wood for a princess's cradle. Then they stacked the wood in sack bags. They heaved the sackbags on their backs and plodded slowly to the castle stamping and singing:

The children stand in two lines, facing each other. Holding hands with a partner opposite, and standing with the right foot forward, they seesaw backward and forward very gently to a pentatonic melody.

"Oh the load in my sack
Is so heavy on my back—
My poor old back
Is just about to crack."

They tipped out the wood and ran back, very quickly, for some more wood—run, run, run—and when they had brought all the wood to the castle, they remembered their tools and ran to bring them back.

The woodcutters carved the cradle. They cut and carved with care a cosy rocking cradle for Princess Briar Rose.

What were all the maidens making? Some were singing and spinning, spinning and singing, while the whirring wheels ran round and round and the whirring wheels ran round.

Repeat several times.

Others were weaving, over and under, and over and under with silver threads and gold.

All the maidens were making garments for Briar Rose. Some were knitting: knit, knit, knit, plain and purl, plain and purl. Some were even walking round the castle while they knitted, singing to themselves:

The children can become threads and move across the circle making patterns. It is lovely to weave in Eurythmy with pentatonic music.

> "Purl and plain
> Purl and plain
> Plain and purl
> Plain and purl."

To thread a needle in Eurythmy: O with thumb and forefinger, and U with thumb and forefinger of the other hand. Push the thread through the hole.

Some maidens were stitching—stitch, stitch, stitch. What were they stitching?

When all the stitch, stitch, stitching was done, it was folded away. When all the plain and purl knitting was done, it was folded away. When all the gold and silver weaving was done, it was folded away. When all the spinning was done, it was wound and washed and wound once more into big balls for weaving, and tidied away. When all the carving was done, the tools were cleaned and laid down carefully.

The children will know what they are stitching; curtains for the cradle, bonnets and coats, mittens and blankets can all be made in Eurythmy.

Then the men and maidens danced in a ring. They danced round the ring to the right, round the ring to the left, up to the middle, the middle, the middle, and back and back again; then round themselves and round themselves, then they all took hands.

After the dance, they stood, tall and straight with feet together, and they wished and they wished a mighty wish for Princess Briar Rose.

The next week, repeat the story in verse. An angel can bring the baby from the stars. The wise fairy women bring their gifts. The story can last through the whole term if each part of the story is done in detail and the following week in verse. The rest of the story is given here in verse form. ("The Basque Fairy Tale" and "The Three Jolly Musicians" can be done in the same way with six-year-old preschool children, or in Grade 1.)

(*Next lesson.*)

The queen she was a-weeping,
　　A-weeping, a-weeping,
The queen she was a-weeping,
　　A-weeping by the pool.

When out there hopped a little frog,
　　A little frog, a little frog,
When out there hopped a little frog,
　　And softly said to her:

A beauteous baby will be born,
　　Will be born, will be born,
A beauteous baby will be born,
　　And her name shall be Briar Rose.

Then all the men went a-cutting wood,
　　A-cutting wood, a-cutting wood,
Then all the men went a-cutting wood,
　　And they carved the baby's cradle.

And all the maidens spun and wove,
　　Spun and wove, spun and wove,
Then all the maidens spun and wove,
　　And they stitched the royal robes.

And when the baby came to earth,
　　Came to earth, came to earth,
And when the baby came to earth,
　　All the world was glad.

Twelve good fairies brought their blessings,
　　Brought their blessings, brought their blessings,
Twelve good fairies brought their blessings,
　　To little Briar Rose.

The thirteenth fairy stamped and raged,
　　Stamped and raged, stamped and raged,
The thirteenth fairy stamped and raged,
　　And cast a wicked spell.

"O Briar Rose shall prick her finger,
　　Prick her finger, prick her finger,
O Briar Rose shall prick her finger,
　　And fall down dead.

She shall not die but sleep and sleep,
　　Sleep and sleep, sleep and sleep,
She shall not die but sleep and sleep,
　　For one hundred years."

When Briar Rose was twelve years old,
　　Twelve years old, twelve years old,
When Briar Rose was twelve years old,
　　She climbed the gloomy tower.

She tried to roll the whirring wheel,
　　Whirring wheel, whirring wheel,
She tried to roll the whirring wheel,
　　And she pricked her little finger.

Then Briar Rose fell deep asleep,
　　Deep asleep, deep asleep,
Then Briar Rose fell deep asleep,
　　And all within those walls.

Then up there grew a prickly hedge,
　　Prickly hedge, prickly hedge,
Then up there grew a prickly hedge,
　　And no one dared go through.

At last a prince came riding by,
　　Riding by, riding by,
At last a prince came riding by,
　　And he drew his shining sword.

He hacked and cut the prickly hedge,
　　Prickly hedge, prickly hedge,
He hacked and cut the prickly hedge,
　　And roses blossomed forth.

"O Briar Rose, awake from sleep,
　　Awake from sleep, awake from sleep,
O Briar Rose awake from sleep,
　　And all within those walls."

And so they all lived happily,
　　Lived happily, lived happily,
And so they all lived happily,
　　For ever, ever after.

This is a summer story. Little children live more closely wrapped up in wind and weather, in spring and summer, autumn, and winter than we do. In autumn there is corn to cut with the farmers. We can go blackberry picking with old Jill and make little gallipots full of jam for the fairies. We can gather flowers and fruit for the Harvest Mother. We can go to the good gardener's house and plant apple pips and watch them grow. We can visit old Mother Crosspatch, who only looks cross but isn't, and do some baking or sweep the whirling, swirling autumn leaves.

In the preschool, the seasons give the tenor of our lessons.

NOTE: In "And Then Take Hands" there are other poems that can be dealt with in this way (namely a detailed story about each verse each lesson). For 4 year olds there is "Over in the Meadow," for older pre-school children or Grade I the Basque Fairy Tale and the Three Jolly Musicians.

Suggestions for Lessons in the Preschool

Fall Lesson

When the Spiders' Webs Are Covered with Dewdrops

There was once a spider, a splendid spider, and she sat in a corner to spin. And she spun and she spun and she spun, and she wove a wonderful web.

The spider watched and she waited, oh she watched and she waited and nobody came.

In the night, the waterfairies flew and they flew and they flew with drops of dew, with drops of dew, pitter patter, pitter patter, pitter patter. They hung the dew drops on the web to make it more wonderful. Then came . . .

The children take turns carrying a silken thread across the circle to each other, then altogether or individually weave it in or out.

u u —

> Little Miss Muffet
> And sat on a tuffet
> Eating her curds and whey—
> There came a big spider
> And she sat down beside her
> And this spider didn't frighten
> Miss Muffet away, away,
> She didn't frighten
> Miss Muffet away.

She whispered so softly:

> "Come and see, come and see
> What the fairies have hung
> On the wonderful web
> That I've spun, I've spun.
> Dew drops like diamonds
> Sparkling in the sun."

Miss Muffet could go and fetch the hippity hoppity rabbits to come and look, and the twittering tom tits, or robin redbreast, or a mouse. Perhaps the children from the preschool class could go hand in hand, through the land, to see the lovely spider webs . . . and so on and on.

Winter Lesson

Winter Is Here

Oh, the king was in his castle
A-shivering with the cold.   **Clapping.**
And the queen was in the castle
A-shivering with the cold.
They clapped their hands (*repeat*)   **Ad lib, stamping one foot,**
They stamped their feet (*repeat*)   **then the other, clapping in**
They skipped around, around, around.   **front, behind and above**
They sang: **the head.**
"Winter is here
For ever and ever.
We will never get warm.
No, not ever."   **Ad lib.**

Little Robin flew, and he flew and he flew and   uu—   **with L**
he flew till he came to the king's castle, and he pecked
at the window, peck, peck, peck, peck, peck, peck and   uu—**with fingers**
began to sing. The king came to the window. The queen
came to the window. They opened the window. Robin
sang:

"Listen, listen, listen
Winter is going away, away.
Spring is coming one day, one day
Soooooooon—soooooooon—soooooooon."

The king said, "What shall we give Robin for bringing   **Ask the children, and give**
this good news?" Then the queen said, "We will give   **Robin whatever they sug-**
him a wife and a wedding feast."   **gest.**

The North Wind*

The North Wind doth blow,
And we shall have snow,
And what will poor Robin do then,
    poor thing?
Oh, he'll fly to the barn
And to keep himself warm,
He'll hide his head under his wing,
    poor thing.

(*Next lesson.*)

The North Wind doth blow,
And we shall have snow,
And what will the children do then,
    poor things?
Oh, when lessons are done,
They'll jump, skip and run,
And play till they get themselves warm,
    poor things!

(*Next lesson.*)

The West Wind doth blow,
And away is the snow,
Now what will poor Robin do then,
    poor thing?
He'll fly where it's best
To build a wee nest
And hide his eggs under his wing,
    poor thing!

Let the North Wind blow in and out of the trees, children taking turns to be the wind, one or two at a time. The others stand in a ring like trees or houses or chimneypots. Then a big snow cloud gathers and scatters snow flakes; softly, softly falls the snow, (contraction, expansion), over the grass, over the trees, over the roofs. Ask the children where else (over our school). The teacher and a child can make a big barn, and the children can go inside to sleep in B. They can take turns flying out to see if the snow has stopped. Then finish the lesson with the poem.

Stamp and clap to get warm. Put on boots and coats. Make a snowman. Roll a ball (R, B), getting it bigger. Then another for the head, and so on. Coal for eyes, carrot for a nose. The sun can come and melt the snowman.

Have a nest-building lesson with eggs hatching, baby birds opening their beaks in uu-saying, "Feed me please, feed me please." Mother bird goes around feeding baby birds.*

Notes for an Advent Lesson

In the morning very early, the children put on their hats and caps, their coats and boots, and they each take a knife, a sharp knife (sharpen it with a uu-). Tramp, tramp, tramp. Tall holly tree with red, red berries. Cut it so carefully, put in a big bag. Find a Christmas tree. Cut, cut, cut. Put branches in a bag. Bundles on our

---

*There are more verses in *The Book of a Thousand Poems,* published by Evan Brothers, Ltd., London.

backs. Go back home and weave an advent wreath. Weaving, weaving in and out. Four candles, 1, 2, 3, 4, no less, no more. Carry wreath to the house of the old woman. Knock, knock, knock . . . open the door and light the candle, sing a carol.

Notes for a Spring Lesson

The Good Gardener

Go to the good gardener's house. Good gardener:

> Digs, digs, digs,
> Rakes, rakes, rakes,
> Sows the seeds, sows the seeds,
> Weeds out the weeds.

Ask the children which flowers they'd like to be in the garden—pansies, tulips, daffodowndillies, daisies.

> We'll go to the gardener, the gardener
> We'll go and see the gardener . . .
> Knock, knock, knock,
> Is anyone at home?

Dance around the room.

Window opens. We say, "Please may we peep at your garden today?" (*repeat*) "And see what we can see?" Gardener says:

> It's all a-blowing and a-growing
> All a-blowing and a-growing
> Pick some flowers to take home.

*   *   *

> Spring is coming,
> Spring is coming,
> Flowers are coming, too.
> Pansies, lilies, daffodillies
> All are coming through.

Midsummer Lesson

Midsummer's Day

Hey, ho Midsummer's Day is not far away. So we'll build up a fire, as high as a spire. Chop, chop, chop. Build a big bonfire with branches and twigs. Flame,

flame, fire, flame. Shoot, sparks, shoot. Crackle branches, crackle. Burn and
blaze, burn and blaze, up to the sky.

> Dance around the fire.
> Go to bed.
> The elfin folk come out to dance: One little elf dances all by himself, then two
> little elves, then three, till all the little elves are dancing.

Hodie, it is Midsummer's Day
Flowers as red as fire,
The Sun can rise no higher,
Hodie, it is Midsummer's Day.

Walking in the Rain

Go for a walk in the rain. Put on boots.

Boys' boots are big,
And when boys jump.
Boy's big boots go
Bump, bump, bump.

*   *   *

How do we walk in the rain?
Splish, splosh, splish, splosh.
How do we walk in the sunshine?
On tippytoes, we dance and sing,
Dance and sing, dance and sing.
How do we walk in the snow?
Slowly, slowly, on we go,
Through the snow, through the snow.
When the rain comes pitter patter,
We run to our homes for shelter.
When the sun comes out again,
We dance and play, in and out, round about.

*   *   *

Rain, rain, go away.
Come again another day.   *or:*
The rain has gone, the sun is out,
Come and play and dance about.

Rain on the green grass,
Rain on the tree,
Rain on the housetops,
BUT NOT ON ME!   **Run into the house.**

Fingerplays

Fingerplays help to make nimble little fingers, capable hands, and versatile minds.

The Little Toad

I am a little toad, Living by the road.	**Right fist rests sheltered by left.**
Beneath a stone I dwell, Snug in a little shell.	
Hip-hip-hop, hip-hip-hop!	**Jump right fist behind left.**

Just listen to my song, I sleep all winter long.	
But in the spring, I peep out, And then I jump and jump about.	**Move right fist from behind left, and have it jump about.**

And now I catch a fly	**Grab with right hand.**
Before he winks an eye. And now I take a hop, And now and then I stop. Hip-hip-hop, hip-hip-hop!	

Penguins

One royal penguin, Nothing much to do, Called for his brother,	**First finger up**
Then there were two!	**Second finger up**

Two royal penguins, Happy as could be, Called for their sister,	
Then they were three!	**Third finger up**

Three royal penguins, Wished there were more, Called for their mother,	
Then there were four.	**Little finger up**

Four royal penguins,
Learning how to dive,
Called for their father,
Then there were five.   **Thumb**

One — two — three — four — five.

The Owl and the Brownies

An owl sat alone
On the branch of a tree,
And he was as quiet   **Sit quietly, hands folded in**
As quiet could be.   **lap.**

It was night and his eyes
Were round, like this.   **Cup hands like semi-**
He looked around; not a   **circles, hold to eyes. Look**
Thing did he miss.   **around.**

Some brownies crept up
On a branch of the tree,   **Fingers of one hand creep**
And they were as quiet   **on back of other hand and**
As quiet could be.   **up arm.**

Said the wise old owl,
"To-whooo! To-whooo!"
Up jumped the brownies,   **Raise both arms, making**
And away they all flew.   **flying movement.**

The owl sat alone
On the branch of a tree,
And he was as quiet   **Sit quietly, hands folded in**
As quiet could be.   **lap.**

Itsy Bitsy Spider

Itsy bitsy spider
Climbed up the water spout.
Down came the rain and washed the spider out.
Out came the sun and dried up all the rain;
Itsy, bitsy spider
Climbed up the spout again.

Right thumb and right index finger climb until they can't go any farther. Then left thumb and left index finger.

Hands

Open, close them,
Open, close them,
Give a little clap.
Open, close them,
Open, close them,
Place them in your lap.

Above head.

Creep them down,
Creep them up,
Way up to your chin.
Open up your little mouth
But do not let them in.

Open, close them,
Open, close them,
Give a little clap.
Open, close them,
Open, close them,
Place them in your lap.

Fold hands together

The Beehive

Here is the beehive,
Where are the bees?
Hidden away where nobody sees.
Here they come creeping
Out of the hive,
One, two, three, four, five.
Buzz, buzz, buzz, buzz.

Out comes the thumb and then the fingers of one hand, while the other hand remains half-closed as the beehive.

Mother Goose Rhymes

Pit, pat, well-a-day!
Little robin flew away.
Where can little robin be?
High up in the cherry tree.

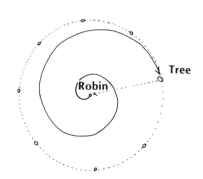

* * *

Down with the lamb,
Up with the lark,

Run to bed, children,
Before it gets dark.

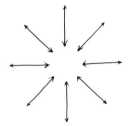

* * *

A little boy went into a barn
And lay down on some hay;
An owl came out and flew about
And the little boy ran away.

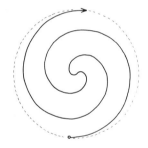

* * *

Hello, little perky bird,
What is your name?
My name is Johnny Sparrow,
Johnny Sparrow is my name.

**"Johnny" flies to another
child, who then stands in
the center of the circle.**

* * *

Five tiny fairies hiding in a flower,
Five tiny fairies caught in a shower.
Daddy Cock-A-Doodle standing on one leg.
Old Mother Speckle-Top lays a golden egg.
Old Mrs. Crosspatch comes with her stick,
Fly away fairies, quick, quick, quick.

Hush-a-bye Bairdie

Scottish

A good rocking song for the end of a Eurythmy lesson

Hush-a-bye bairdie, croon, croon, Hush-a-bye bairdie,

croon, croon, The sheep are gane to the silver wood, And the

cows are gone to the broom, broom. It's braw milking the

kye, kye, It's braw milking the kye, The birds are

singing, the bells are ringing, The wild deer come galloping

by, by.

And hush-a-ba bairdie, croon, croon,
Hush-a-ba bairdie, croon,
The gaits are gane to the mountain hie,
And they'll no be hame till noon, noon.

Minnie and Winnie

Lord Alfred Tennyson

Minnie and Winnie
Slept in a shell.
Sleep, little ladies!
And they slept well.

Pink was the shell within,
Silver without;
Sounds of the great sea
Wander'd about.

Sleep, little ladies!
Wake not soon!
Echo on echo
Dies to the moon.

Two bright stars
Peep'd into the shell
"What are they dreaming of?
Who can tell?"

Started a green linnet
Out of the croft;
Wake, little ladies,
The sun is aloft!

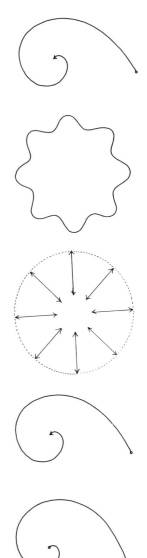

Verses for Beginning or Ending Eurythmy Lessons

On Mother Earth
W. M. von Heider

On Mother Earth I stand upright,
The sun above by day gives light,
The moon and stars by night.

Guarded from Harm
Anonymous

Guarded from harm;
Cared for by angels;
Here stand we,
Loving and bold,
Truthful and good.

Summer Verse
George Macdonald

The lightning and thunder
They go and they come;
But the stars and the stillness
Are always at home.

The Sun Above
Ilse Tupaj

The Sun above,
The Earth below,
We love them both
Where e'r we go.

The Sun Warms
Elizabeth Edmunds

The sun warms Mother Earth
And fills the world with light.

I Reverence

**Elizabeth Baumann,
translated by W. M. von Heider**

I reverence the heavens,
I reverence the earth,
I reverence my fellow men,
A guardian angel keeps me.

I Am a Man

Ilse Tupaj

I am a man,
I help where I can.

The Earth Is Sure

Elizabeth Edmunds

The earth is sure beneath my feet,
And, see, upright I stand,
The heavens arch above my head,
My friends are here on either hand.

Birds in the Air

Angelus Silesius

Birds in the air,
Stones on the land,
Fishes in water,
I'm in God's hand.

Christmas (I)

W. M. von Heider

Ah, dark is the sky;
Oh, cold is the earth;
A light I will be
At the Christ Child's birth.

Christmas Verse
W. M. von Heider

In the darkest night
The earth shall be light
And shall gleam like a star.

You and I, I and you,
We will give our light too.

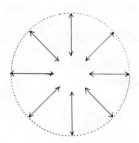

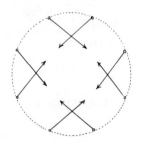

Christmas (II)
W. M. von Heider

Lullaby, lullaby, Holy Child,
The kingdoms of earth
Salute thy birth.

Lullaby, lullaby, Holy Child,
The lily, the rose, and the Christmas tree,
The birds and beasts and busy bee,
All bring their gifts, oh child, to thee.

Lullaby, lullaby, Holy Child,
A little starry light I bring,
Which is of my own making.

Closing Verse
Anon.

Sun, moon, and stars
Shining wide and far;
Over land, over sea,
Over you, over me,
For my soul's delight
Shine into my heart.

Verses for I A O

Collected from Waldorf Teachers

I am here,
Here we are,
We love each other so.

We are strong,
Strong are we.

Where are you all?
Here we
   are.
Good morning, big wide world.

Straight as a spear I stand.
Strength fills my legs and arms.
Warm is my heart with love.

Who are you all?
We are gnomes;
Gnomes are we.

See here is my head,
See how strong my legs are,
See how much love my heart can hold.

Here stand we,
Firm and free.
From afar
Shines our star.
In our hearts,
We enfold
Sungold.

Here stand we,
Straight as spears.
Strength in our arms and legs,
Warmth in our hearts
And love for our work
In the world.

Chapter Two

Grades One and Two (Ages Six to Eight)

During these two years, the children learn to experience forms, straight and curved. They learn to write and to read. They learn something of the quality of numbers and the four rules of arithmetic. They learn French and German songs and poems. And they learn to knit and crochet.

Eurythmy Lessons with Grade 1

How does it feel to be six years old? How does it feel to be in Grade 1?

It was in January, the first snow had fallen. A child came skipping up to me with arms outspread: "Wouldn't you love to be a tree?" Before I could answer, she danced away singing, "I'm a tree. I'm a tree with snow on my branches. It is so lovely to be a tree with snow on my branches."

It was lunchtime. There were apples for dessert. "Please peel my apple"; "And mine"; "And mine."

"The skin is the best part."

"My mummy says that too, but please peel my apple and cut it the magic way."

Patiently, I peeled all the little apples and cut them the magic way. When I looked up, not only the apples but also the skin had been eaten! Of course, it is impossible to bite into an apple without a front tooth and a wobbler down below.

Time

"I've got a birthday on Sunday!"

"I wish I had. I have to wait longer than anybody for my birthday."

"Why?"

"Because my birthday's right at the end of the year, after Christmas."

Space

A six-year-old in the bath: "Look, what long legs I've got. They reach right up to my tummy."

The children are full of imagination, each one is a Proteus. They not only imitate; they actually become trees, birds, stones. They can even creep inside forms—inside straight lines and curves! The children dance, jump, skip, and run. They delight in movement.

Between the ages of six and seven, the children are changing their teeth. They live in the element of time, of rhythm, of becoming, of growing. It is the building of the house, the finding and lashing together of sticks to make a tent, the digging of the cave, the building of the castle that is more important than living in the finished house, tent, or cave. When a garden, a house, a shop is finished, the game is usually over.

The children in Grade 1 are celebrating their second birthday. Their physical body was born at birth. At seven, the body of formative forces—their etheric body—is born. The change of teeth marks this new birth. In order to help children dwell happily within their bodies, we must lead them into the realms of form and metamorphosis, using their natural abilities—those of imagination, love of movement, repetition, and rhythm. It is not only to help them write well that the curriculum specifies straight lines, curves, and pattern drawing. It is essential that the teacher realize the necessity to develop this feeling for form. Just to draw patterns and run straight lines is not enough. This is like copying writing and being unable to read and understand the meaning. Rudolf Steiner comments as follows:

> You may remember the lecture in which I tried to awaken a sense for the origin of the acanthus leaf. I explained that it is not true that the leaf of the acanthus plant had been copied, as is related in the legend. The truth is that the acanthus leaf arose from an inner formative impulse. Later, people thought, "It resembles nature, it resembles the leaf of the acanthus plant." But it had not been copied from nature—we must bear this in mind when drawing and painting. Then, at last, there will be an end to the fearful error which devastates human minds so sadly. When people see something man has made, they say either, "It looks very natural; it is a good copy" or, "It looks very unnatural." It is not important to judge whether a good imitation of nature has been achieved or not. Resemblance to the external world should appear as something secondary.
>
> What must live in man is an inner growing together with the forms themselves, an ability to live within the form. Even when drawing a nose, one must experience an inner relationship with the form of the nose itself. Only later does the resemblance result. One would never be able to awaken an understanding, an inner sense for form between the ages of seven and fourteen merely by copying forms externally. One must be conscious of the inner creative element that can be developed between the ages of seven and fourteen. If one misses the development of these creative forces at this time, it can never be made good later in life. The forces which are active at this time die away and, at the best, one can only get a "makeshift," unless a transformation of the individual takes place through what we call an "initiation," natural or unnatural.*

It is of great importance at this time to strive for an understanding of the language of form; to experience inwardly the movement and forms of the plant world, the movements between leaves, between bud and flower, fruit and seed. For instance, watch a bluebell from the moment the first green upright shoot comes through the soil. See how the flower bells gradually turn down to look at the earth, and then lift up

---

*The Practical Course for Teachers, Chapter 1, Anthroposophic Press, New York 1937.

their seed cups again to the sky. It is to this awareness of the movement of the formative forces that Dr. Steiner refers in Lecture 1.[†]

He describes how the acanthus leaf motif of the Corinthian columns is a metamorphosis of the palmette or sun motif of the Dorian columns, not an imitation of the acanthus plant.

It is said that Callimachos, the Corinthian sculptor, had seen a basket surrounded by acanthus leaves, and the idea of the Corinthian column came to him. Dr. Steiner tells the legend in its entirety. He describes how Callimachos was able to see clairvoyantly the sun motif struggling with the earth motif over the grave of a Corinthian girl. Over the grave was hovering the etheric body of the girl. The forms of the Greek capitols were created purely out of the spirit.

We must endeavor, as teachers, to seek for artistic understanding of form so that we can strengthen the child's inner sense of the movement of form in these early years.

Helen Keller gives a wonderful description of the flow of curved and straight lines:

> My world is built of touch sensations, devoid of physical color and sound; but without color and sound it breathes and throbs with life.
>
> The coolness of a waterlily rounding into bloom is different from the coolness of an evening wind in summer, and different again from the coolness of the rain that soaks into the hearts of growing things and gives them life and body. The hardness of the rock is to the hardness of wood what a man's deep bass is to a woman's voice when it is low. What I call beauty I find in certain combinations of all these qualities, and is largely derived from the flow of curved and straight lines which is over all things.
>
> Eloquence to the touch resides not in straight lines, but in unstraight lines, or in many curved and straight lines together. They appear and disappear, are now deep, now shallow, now broken off or lengthened or swelling. They rise and sink beneath my fingers, they are full of sudden starts and pauses, and their variety is inexhaustible and wonderful.
>
> My fingers cannot, of course, get the impression of a large whole at a glance; but I feel the parts, and my mind puts them together.
>
> The process reminds me of the building of Solomon's temple, where was neither saw, not hammer, nor any tool heard while the stones were laid one upon another. The silent worker is imagination which decrees reality out of chaos.
>
> Twofold is the miracle when, through my fingers, my imagination reaches forth and meets the imagination of an artist which he has embodied in a sculptured form. Although, compared with the life-warm, mobile face of a friend, the marble is cold and pulseless and unresponsive, yet it is beautiful to my hand. Its flowing curves and bendings are a real pleasure; only breath is wanting; but under the spell of the imagination the marble thrills and becomes the divine reality of the ideal. Imagination puts a sentiment into every line and curve, and the statue in my touch is indeed the goddess herself who breathes and moves and enchants.[*]

And Frank Lloyd Wright throws a different light on straight lines and curves:

> A light blanket of snow fresh-fallen over sloping fields, gleaming in the morning

---

[†]"Ways to a New Style in Architecture," Anthroposophic Press, New York 1927.

[*]*The Seeing Hand,*

sun. Clusters of pod-topped weeds woven of bronze here and there sprinkling the spotless expanse of white. Dark sprays of slender metallic straight lines, tipped with quivering dots. Pattern to the eye of the sun, as the sun spread delicate network of more pattern in blue shadows on the white beneath.

"Come, my boy," said Uncle John to his sister Anna's nine-year-old. "Come now, and I will show you how to go!"

Taking the boy by the hand he pulled his big hat down over his shock of gray hair and started straight across and up the sloping fields toward a point upon which he had fixed his keen blue eyes.

Neither to right nor to left, intent upon his goal, straight forward he walked— possessed.

But soon the boy caught the play of naked weed against the snow, sharp shadows laced in blue arabesque beneath. Leaving his mitten in the strong grasp, he got free.

He ran first left, to gather beads on stems and then beads and tassels on more stems. Then right, to gather prettier ones. Again—left, to some darker and more bril-liant—and beyond to a low-spreading kind. Farther on again to tall golden lines tipped with delicate clusters of dark bronze heads. Eager, trembling, he ran to and fro behind Uncle John, his arms growing full of "weeds."

A long way up the slope, arrived at the point on which he had fixed, Uncle John turned to look back.

A smile of satisfaction lit the strong Welsh face. His tracks in the snow were straight as any string could be straight.

The boy came up, arms full, face flushed, glowing.

He looked up at his uncle—see what he had found!

A stern look came down on him. The lesson was to come. Back there was the long, straight, mindful, heedless line Uncle John's own feet had purposefully made. He pointed to it with pride. And there was the wavering, searching, heedful line embroidering the straight one like some free, engaging vine as it ran back and forth across it. He pointed to that too—with gentle reproof.

Both stood looking back. The small hand with half-frozen fingers was again in its mitten in the older, stronger hand; an indulgent, benevolent smile down now on the shamed young face.

And, somehow, there was something . . . not clear.

Uncle John's meaning was plain—*neither to right nor to the left, but straight, is the way.*

The boy looked at his treasure and then at Uncle John's pride, comprehending more than Uncle John meant he should.

The boy was troubled. Uncle John had left out something that made all the difference.*

*Prelude to Frank Lloyd Wright's Autobiography

The Water of Life
Story for experiencing straight lines and curves.

There was once a great kingdom. It was so great the sun had to stretch its rays to reach to the uttermost ends of it.

Begin with a close circle. Expand it as the run rises, contract as the sun sets.

But when the sun went down and the people returned to their houses, the king to his castle, the huntsman to his lodge, the farmer to his farm, the horses to their stables, the dogs to their kennels, the birds to their nests, the children slept in their cradles and all the world slept until the sun rose in the morning.

Then the children clambered out of their cradles, the birds flew out of their nests, the dogs ran out of their kennels, the horses out of their stables, the farmer from his farm, the huntsman from his lodge, and the king from his castle.*

One day the sun did not want to rise, the animals did not want to go a-galloping, the farmers stayed in their farmhouses, and all the world was sad and dark. Why? Because the king, the well-beloved king, was dying.

Whisper this to the close circle of children.

Louder.

uu—uu—uu—uu—

Up spoke the prince, "Only the Water of Life will heal my father, the king. I will go forth and seek the Water of Life."

So he got on his horse and he galloped away, galloped away, galloped away. When he came to the mountain, did he gallop? No, he climbed down from his horse and led it slowly, slowly, slowly up the steep and rocky mountain path. When he got to the top then he trotted his horse to the valley below, to the valley below, tritt tritt trot.

Galloping rhythm along winding paths — with music.

_ _ _

Walking on long beats with music.

uu—   uu—

Suddenly he stopped. Why? There was a great roaring, rushing, raging river. It was winding and twisting and swirling in his way.

R

"Shall we follow it and look for a bridge?" he wondered, winding in and winding out, winding hither, winding thither and winding round about. Here was a bridge, but too narrow to cross. It was only as wide as a spear. Who would dare to walk over to the land on the other side?

"Stretch out your arms," he said to himself. "Don't look at the water. Look straight ahead at the tower on the top of the hill. Can you see a princess looking out of the window? Keep your eyes on the princess and be brave."

There is no need to chalk a line for the bridge. The children will see it in their imagination.

Go quietly to the other side of the room and hold out your hands to help each child. Give a great cheer when they arrive safely. The children will watch each other and wait for their turns. Often melancholy children will feel it is too difficult — they can't face the ordeal of crossing

(*This could be the end of a lesson.*)

---

*These lessons were given to a particularly noisy, scattered Grade 1. Such children need repetition forward and backward. Rudolf Steiner gave the following exercise for such children: tree, root, trunk, branch, twig, leaf, flower, fruit, to be repeated forward and backward, or man, head, chest, arms, and so on.

that bridge. Let them stay on the "other" bank and give them something important to do, such as looking after the prince's horse—a very special task! Maybe they will dare to cross the river before the prince's journey is over.

When the prince had crossed the raging, roaring, rushing river, he came to a magic wood. He didn't know it was magic until he came out of it. Off we go to the magic wood—into the wood, out of the wood, in and out of the wood again.

The children should hold hands except for the leader and the last one in line. When the children have come out of the spiral, they will have their backs to the center of the circle and will have to go in and out again in order to be the right way round facing the center.

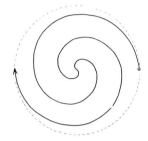

At last he came to the castle. He looked up, he looked down, he looked all around, but there was no door, only a rickety ladder.

Near the ladder lived a witch wife—she couldn't cross the straight and narrow bridge—she could only go slinking slyly, slinking slyly.

If the prince kicked a rung of the ladder it would ring out like a bell and the sly, slinky witch wife would turn him into a toadstool or a stone.

The prince sang to himself, "What's the good of being clever if you're clumsy!" and he climbed to the top of the tower.

Space rods out evenly like a ladder.

The children run as quickly as possible up the ladder to the princess, but if they knock a rod then that "prince" is turned into a toadstool. They can be rescued by another prince who is brave enough to go up the ladder without touching a rung and down again. Then the two princes go together to the top of the tower.

(The lesson could end here.)

The princess led the prince to a cavern below the castle. "There is the well of the Water of Life! Beside it is a golden bowl filled to the brim. You must carry it out of the darkness into the light without spilling a drop." The prince sprinkled himself and the princess with water so that the witch wife could not harm them.

Fill a copper bowl with clear cold water and let the children take turns carrying the bowl. It is a real experience to carry the cold metal. The children will do threefold walking naturally. The teacher must always replace the bowl in the center of the circle. The mood is broken if a child replaces it. It is enough if 4 or 5 children have a turn during a lesson.

They went down the rickety ladder together, through the magic wood, over the spearlike bridge together, along the rushing river together, up the mountain, down into the valley, back to the king and they said:

(Two children.)

"We have dared and endured danger and darkness.
  Deep, deep down underground
  Beyond a far-away, far-away forest
  A glittering golden goblet gleamed
  In a cavern cut in the castle rock—
  We have carried that cup with care to our king,
  For health and healing lie hidden therein."

Calming consonants
DFGKH.

Then the king drank the Water of Life and was healed.

Then the sun could rise and stretch its rays to the uttermost parts of the kingdom, and the people went singing into the fields, the animals went a-galloping, the birds a-flying, and all the world was glad. When the sun went down, the people returned to their houses, the king to his castle, the huntsman to his lodge, the farmer to his farm, the horses to their stables, the dogs to their kennels, the birds to their nests, the bees to their hives, and the children slept in their cradles, and they all lived happily ever after.

The children are quiet for a whole minute at the end of the lesson. Before dismissing them, tell them who will be the leader next week and who will be the last in line and close the door when the lesson begins.

Suggestion for a Grade I Eurythmy Lesson

Jack and the Bean Stalk

Who lives in this little house? A poor woman sits a-weeping, a-weeping, a-weeping.

Jack: "Mother why are you weeping?"
Mother: "We have no money,
            Not even a penny,
            And nothing to sell,
            No bread in the bin,
            No flour and no meal.

            We must sell our cow.
            Brush cow's coat till it shines
            Brush, brush, brush.
            Come on Rosy. Munch, munch, moooo."

Jack: "I'm going to market."

Jack meets an old woman:

            "Give me your cow and take this bean,
            Take this bean so brown.
            It is better than silver,
            Better than gold,
            Better than the king's own crown."

Jack takes the bean and runs home happily.

Mother: "You're a bad, bad boy,   **Stamping and clapping
            A bad, bad boy,   round in a circle.**
            A bad, bad boy."

Mother flings the bean through the window. In the night the bean begins to grow . . . one little leaf, another little leaf getting bigger and bigger.
     Practice straight lines and curves, how the tree grows tall and straight, and the beans wind in and out. Continue the story in this way.

Copper Rod Exercises

Rod exercises are an essential part of the Eurythmy curriculum in the middle and upper school. They should be regarded as very special and used sparingly with the younger children. I have found it better to use rods more as "copper ointment" to enliven the children's arms and hands in Grades 1, 2, and 3.

Rods can be carried upright as birthday candles. They can be rolled up and down the arms as squirrels running up and down the branches of a tree. They can be a magic ladder, or the candlesticks over which Jack jumps in the rhyme:

> Jack be nimble,
> Jack be quick,
> Jack jump over
> The candlestick.

In Grade 1, rods can be the stile over which the crooked man climbed when he found a crooked sixpence. They can even be the trays of cakes from the baker's man, which must be carried with care to the wedding feast.

Grade 2

The Eurythmy lessons in Grade 2 can be planned in the same rhythmical, imaginative way as in Grade 1. Legends and fables can take the place of fairy stories. Now is the time for the children to learn the movements for the consonants and vowels consciously. Their class teacher has taught them to write with love and care; each letter has been a living experience and is still a picture world to them. Children generally "know" the secret of movement and sound before the Eurythmist tells them.

Each sound should be taught in an imaginative way with the correct beginning or impulse (*Ansatz*). It is essential that Eurythmy teachers occupy themselves again with the Eurythmy figures when they are laying the first foundations for the sounds with the children.

Sometimes the evolutionary sequence is taught. Pauline Wehrle has suggested the outline of a story that can be enlarged upon. The evolutionary sequence—the Eurythmy alphabet—can also bring a new experience to the older children when the consonants and vowels are revised at a different level.

Grade 2 children delight in moving in turn the sounds of their own names in Eurythmy. They are eager to find out, for instance, if they have a "wave" (V) in their names. These are the lucky ones—David, Veronica, Ivan, and Valerie. Others have a "light" or "healing leaf" (L) in their names—Valerie again, and Lucy, Alan, Kathleen, Elizabeth, and so on. In our lessons, the "helper" was always allowed to stand in the middle of the circle at the end of the lesson and "eurythmie" someone's name for the others to guess. When everyone's name had been transformed into movement, wonderful words like billowing, whisper, munch, thunder, star, jam, tree, blossom were chosen by the children and transformed into movement.

We were like soothsayers of old reading omens, like explorers discovering new territories. When we "read" Eurythmy, the name James, for instance, would read as follows:

J   tells of one who presses hard against resistance and struggles to overcome difficulties and dissolve them.

A (ā)   tells of one who is awake and aware of danger, of one who is careful and brave.

M   tells of one who is mighty in magic, but can make himself small. He can breathe through, move into, listen to, and understand everything in the world.

S   tells of one who has command of himself and the winds, waves, and storms. One who knows the secret language of the birds and beasts.

James was no longer so pale and small when his name had been read in Eurythmy.

By the end of Grade 2, the children will be able to transform the sounds of a poem into movement without the help of their teacher. The period of learning through imitation is coming to an end.

Symmetrical form drawing—making mirror patterns—is of great importance in these early years, especially in Grades 2 and 3. Drawing or moving a symmetrical form is a process of conscious balancing, which involves the whole being of the child.

The formative forces that manifest themselves in symmetry complete part of their work with dentition, which in itself is a pattern of symmetry. Should the work of the formative forces be delayed or become disorganized, a lack of coordination will become apparent at about the child's ninth year. The balance between the left and right side will be disturbed and if the children can write at all, they will write mirrored letters and numbers (b-d, u-n, p-q, and so on); if they can read, they will read "saw" instead of "was," or maybe they will only be able to read writing upside down. This disability is known as dyslexia. It is becoming more and more prevalent among children today.

Much can be done to prevent this disruption, this retardation, this not wanting to grow up, this resistance to coming down to earth by children, before their ninth year, by drawing and moving symmetrical forms, "mirror patterns."

There are many ways in which this can be done. The Curve of Cassini, for instance, can be experienced around two foci "burning points" at first by the whole class so that the complete form is always a visible movement, then by two children, always opposite each other, then by four children, and so on, while the rest of the class sit down and watch. The children should be told this is a very special form and that when they are in Grade 9 they will meet it again and learn to draw it, to construct it. It may take a whole term until they have learned to balance each other.

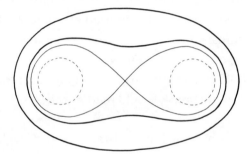

We have run this pattern and other mirror patterns in the untrodden snow in winter. Once on a hot summer's day, the children took off their shoes and socks and two by two dipped their feet in a tub of water; then ran mirror patterns. Their wet footprints remained just long enough for us to see if the patterns reflected each other truly, or if they were top-heavy.

When two children run patterns, however simple these patterns be, we must experience them as a living movement that arises between the two children, an expansion and contraction, a flowing in time, *not* a line in space. This is often easier for children than it is for adults, since children still have the ability to experience form from inside. Children will watch in wonder as new forms arise between them. If two more children join the line, when the space between 1 and 2 contracts, it will expand between 2 and 3 (see diagram).

More pairs can join in until the whole class is moving in two lines facing each other, mirroring in all directions.

When the children are in their ninth year, they can do exercises of coordination. There are many involving movements of the right arm and right leg in alternating connections with the left arm and left leg.

The children can be led to do movements behind their backs, which the teacher does in front for them to see.

These exercises, together with the symmetrical forms, help to bring about a healthy balance in the child's development.

Poems and Songs

Song for the Beginning of Eurythmy Lessons in Grades 1, 2 and 3

Elizabeth Baumann,
Free translation by W. M. von Heider

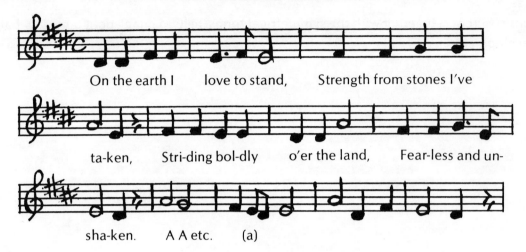

On the earth I love to stand, Strength from stones I've

ta-ken, Stri-ding bol-dly o'er the land, Fear-less and un-

sha-ken. A A etc. (a)

And in water's silvery waves
Gladly do I revel.
From the fishes I can learn
Up and down to travel.
E E etc. (ā)

Upward to the light I look
Where the sun shines brightly,
And with rainbow colors clear
Paints the flowers lightly.
I I (ē)

In the air I love to jump,
Oh! that I were flying
Like a bird with outspread wings
O'er the hilltops gliding.
Ei Ei (I)

Gratefully your gifts I hold
In my heart's deep shrine,
Earth and water, air and light,
Oh, Brothers all of mine.
O O (Ō)

Sun
Eileen Hutchins

O sun, so bright,
Thou givest thy light
And warming love
From Heaven above,
That life on earth
May come to birth.

May our eyes shine
With light like thine;

May our hearts know
Thy warming glow;
May our hands give
Such strength to live;
That we may be
A sun like thee.

The Sun Says
Eileen Hutchins

The sun says, "I glow";
The wind says, "I blow";
The stream says, "I flow";
The tree says, "I grow";
And man says, "I know."

Sunny Bank
Traditional Carol

As I sat on a sunny bank,
A sunny bank, a sunny bank,
As I sat on a sunny bank,
On Christmas Day in the morning.

I spied three ships come sailing by,
Come sailing by, come sailing by,
I spied three ships come sailing by,
On Christmas Day in the morning.

And who should be with those three ships,
With those three ships, with those three ships,
And who should be with those three ships,
But Joseph and his fair lady!

O he did whistle, and she did sing,
And she did sing, and she did sing,
O he did whistle, and she did sing,
On Christmas Day in the morning.

And all the bells on earth did ring,
On earth did ring, on earth did ring,
And all the bells on earth did ring,
On Christmas Day in the morning.

For joy that our Savior he was born,
He was born, he was born,
For joy that our Savior he was born,
On Christmas Day in the morning.

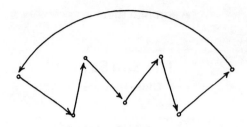

Christmas
Pauline Wehrle

A! A! A!   à
We shepherds see the star;
We wonder at its light so bright
That shines o'er Bethlehem this night.
  A! A! A!

E! E! E!   ā
We shepherds greet the day;
We heard the angels song so sweet;
Our hearts leap up this child to greet.
  E! E! E!

I! I! I!   ē
We go the Child to see,
We'll follow where the star doth lead,
Its light is all we shepherds need.
  I! I! I!

Ei! Ei! Ei!   ī
Behold where He doth lie;
Mary and Joseph there abide;
An ox and ass on either side.
  Ei! Ei! Ei!

O! O! O!   ō
Before Him we bow low
To Jesus born from Heaven above,

We bring our presents and our love.
O! O! O!

U! U! U!
The light I pass to you.
For from the manger's cradle small
Shines forth a flame that lights us all.
U! U! U!

ōō

Words from an Old Spanish Carol

Translated by Ruth Sawyer

Shall I tell you who will come
To Bethlehem on Christmas Morn,
Who will kneel them gently down
Before the Lord, newborn?

One small fish from the river,
With scales of red, red gold,
One wild bee from the heather,
One gray lamb from the fold,
One ox from the high pasture,
One black bull from the herd,
One goatling from the far hills,
One white, white bird.

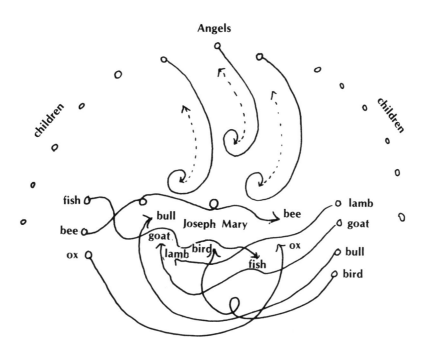

And many children—God give them grace,
Bringing tall candles to light Mary's face.

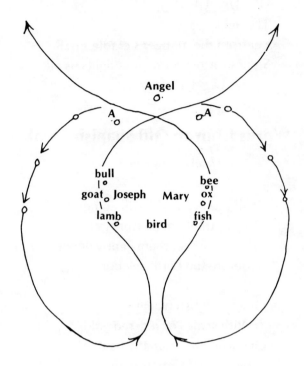

**Eurythmy rods make
beautiful shining candles**

Shall I tell you who will come
To Bethlehem on Christmas Morn,
Who will kneel them gently down
Before the Lord, new-born?

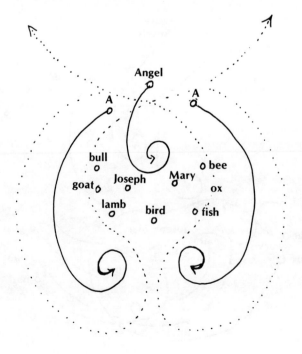

Verses for Spirals

Rosemary Gebert

Softly, softly in I creep,
Where no one else can come:
Out and out and out I speed
To greet the golden sun!

Slowly, softly in I creep,
All by myself, alone:
Out and out and out I speed,
Hello everyone!

Slowly, softly in I creep,
Nobody's here but me;
Out and out and out I speed
Till all my friends I see!

Slowly, softly in I creep,
Tight as a bud I'm curled;
Cock-a-doodle! cries the cock,
Good morning, lovely world!

Up and Down

George Macdonald

The sun is gone down,
And the moon's in the sky;
But the sun will come up,
And the moon be laid by.

The flower is asleep,
But it is not dead;
When the morning shines
It will lift its head.

When winter comes,
It will die—no, no;
It will only hide
From the frost and snow.

Sure is the summer
Sure is the sun;
The night and the winter—
Away they run!

Seeing

Anonymous

I see the sun,
The sun sees me.
I see the moon,
The moon sees me.
I see my star,
My star sees me.
I see you and
You see me.

What the Leaves Said

Anonymous

The leaves said, "It's spring;
  And here are we,
Opening and stretching
  On every tree."

The leaves said, "It's summer;
  Each bird has a nest;
We make the shadow
  Where they can rest."

The leaves said, "It's autumn;
  We are all gay."
Scarlet and golden
  And russet were they.

The leaves said, "It's winter;
  Weary are we."
So they lay down and slept
  Under the tree.

Easter Song

Morwenna Bucknall

From the hills flow the streamlets,
And laughing they say:
    "Now Easter is coming and spring's on the way."

Hear the birdies are calling
And laughing they say:
    "Now Easter is coming and spring's on the way."

See the green shoots are sprouting,
And laughing they say:
    "Now Easter is coming and spring's on the way."

The flowers are ringing their bells and they say:
    "The sun and the wind and the rain and the earth
    Sing Easter is coming, and springtime is here."

From the hills flow the streamlets,
And laughing they say:
    "Now Easter is coming and spring's on the way.
    The sun and the wind and the rain and the earth
    Sing Easter is coming and springtime is here."

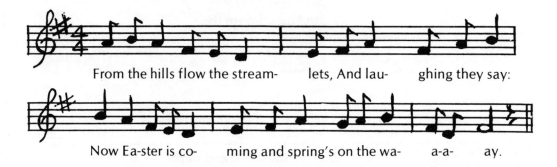

Last verse (last 2 lines):

Easter
Anonymous

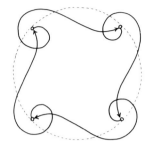

Waken sleeping butterfly,
Burst your narrow prison,
Spread your golden wings and fly
For the sun is risen,
Spread your wings and tell the story
How he arose, the King of Glory.

Butterflies
W. M. von Heider

Caterpillars:
Here we come
Creepy-creep,
Half-asleep.

Chrysalis:
We'll spin ourselves
A silken bed,
Brown and dead.

Butterflies:
Fly away
Through the skies,
Butterflies.

Midsummer
Rosemary Gebert

By summer enchanted,
The green earth lies sleeping,
A fairy-tale princess
Who's under a spell.

Laugh! You'll not wake her,
Shout! You'll not shake her,
Princess, sleep well!

Her children of dream grow
In beauty around her,
In butterfly, blossom
And brown furry bee.

They cannot wake her,
Who then can shake her?
From drowsy dream wake her?
Who can it be?

When green corn grows golden
And blossoms are seeding,
A prince will come riding
Earthward his way.

A star-prince will take her,
With meteors shake her,
From deep sleep awake her,
One bright autumn day.

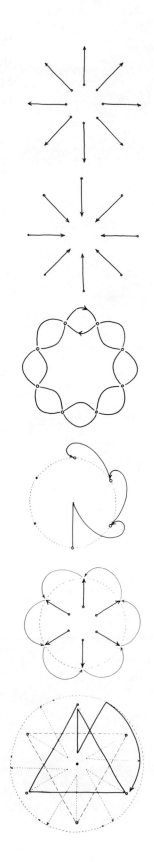

Dummling's Song

Joan Marcus

Walk along, skip along, dance along with me;
I have found a golden goose under the roots of a tree.
Walk along, skip along, dance along with me.

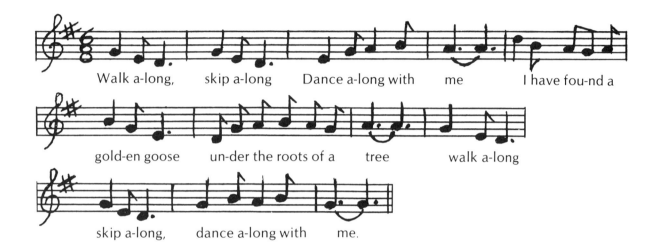

Song of the Twelve Dancing Princesses

W. M. von Heider

Magic door   Trundle bed,
Open wide,   Rise once more,
Trundle bed,   Swiftly close
Downward glide!   Magic door!

Stepping Stones

Traditional

Stepping over stepping stones,
One, two, three,
Stepping over stepping stones,
Come with me!
The river's very fast,
The river's very wide,
And we'll step across on stepping stones
And reach the other side.

Jumping over Rods
Anapest

Pease pudding hot,
Pease pudding cold,
Pease pudding in the pot
Nine days old.
Some like it hot,
Some like it cold,
Some like it in the pot
Nine days old.

My Mother Said
Anapest

My mother said, I never should
Play with the gypsies in the wood:
If I did, she would say;
"Naughty [child's name] to disobey!"

The children stand facing each other on the circle. They clap hands together in rhythm and then pass on to meet the next child in the circle, saying, "Goodbye to you and welcome to you."

The Wild Beast
Anapest
Translated from a German folk song
by W. M. von Heider

We will go for a walk in our garden fair
To see what we can see;
I've heard it said there's a wild beast there
Who will gobble up you and me.
When will he come?

anapest

Not at one,
Not at two,
Not at three,
Not at four,
Not at five,
Not at six,
Not at seven,
Not at eight,
Not at nine,
Not at ten,
At eleven he knocks!
At twelve he comes!

Verse
**for moving from straight lines into a curved form
without a pause
W. M. von Heider**

Four strong walls
Has this castle of ours:
Parapets, pinnacles,
Turrets and towers;
And a glorious garden full of flowers.

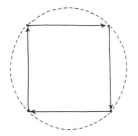

The Adventurous Fellow

**Pauline Wehrle
Evolutionary sequence**

He bears a burden in a sack,   **B**
He bears a bundle on his back.

He will go forth and meet   **M**
What he has to meet,
Be it a mountain or be it a mouse
Or a mighty magician in his house.

Do you dare? Yes I do!   **D**
Are you bold? Good for you!

Now what is this? I am curious to know!   **N**
That is enough! To another I go!

Beware of the spell that will roll you away,   **R**
Let you neither rest nor stay.

In the shelter of the trees   **L**
He can linger, take his ease.

Now let me go through the great gateway.   **G**
Go, do not stay — get out of my way!

Breathe the fresh air   **CH**
In huge gulps, crystal clear.

I have now the strength to free my friend,   **F**
With fiery finger my force to send.

He wins a magic secret   S
That can do a good spell.
Wild wolf be still!
Wild bear be still!

Who'll give his help?   H
I'll give my help!

And for his courage of great renown   T
He wins a treasure and golden crown.

Stories and Legends

These stories and legends—about flowers, birds, and insects—are particularly appropriate for Eurythmy lessons in Grades 1 and 2, but many could also be performed by older classes for festivals.

Suggestion for Grade 2:

The Cloud

There once was a summer, so hot, so hot, so hot, that all things withered, all things withered and withered away.

> The stout oaks withered.
> The poplars perished.
> The celandine died.
> The dandelions and daisies shriveled.
> The brown beeches were burnt.
> The green grass was scorched.   **contraction**
> The cattle were killed by sunstroke.
> The rivers and streams ceased to flow, and disappeared.
> And all men prayed: "Send us rain."
> But no rain fell.

At long last a little cloud heard the call of the thirsty earth, and it sailed, and it sailed, and it sailed through the sky, and it sailed, and it sailed, and it sailed. And it swelled, and it swelled, and it swelled with pity for the poor earth. "If I let my raindrops fall, I shall be no more a lovely cloud. I shall be nothing, nothing, nothing," said the cloud.

    (Ask the children in turn: What would you do if you were a cloud?)

> The beautiful big cloud broke.
> Rain fell on the thirsty earth.
> The people drank and were grateful.
> The streams and rivers began to flow,
> The cattle were no longer killed by sunstroke.
> The scorched grass grew green again.   **expansion**
> The brown beeches grew buds and leaves.
> The dandelions and daisies flowered.
> The celandines opened golden petals.
> The poplars stood upright.
> The stout oaks grew sturdy and strong.
> And life came back to the earth.

The Legend of the Scabious

In the beginning, when God created the flowers, He created one plant full of healing. In the root lay the healing.

Now the devil liked to plague people and make them cross and angry. "I will plague them with spots, I will plague them with spots." He would point at   uu— them from behind a bush and spots would appear, scabs and sores.

The Angel of the Lord came down and showed the people the healing plant. They dug, and they dug, and they dug the deep roots and boiled them in milk and drank the milk and were healed.

The Devil was very angry. "I will bite off the root, I will bite off the root of   uu—uu— that healing plant," (*clapping and stepping*). So he bit off the root, and that is why it is called "the Devil's-bit scabious." But there is a lot of healing still in the little bit of root that is left.

Cowslips

Long ago, Saint Peter was leaning over the gate of Heaven, gazing down upon the earth, when his golden keys fell from his hand. Down, down, down they dropped to the dark earth below—gone from his gaze.

As he could not leave his labor as guardian of the gate of Heaven, Saint Peter sought the service of the angels. At once one of the smallest of the angels went winging his way to earth.

Saint Peter stood gazing down from the golden gateway. He watched and waited. But the little angel did not return and was lost to sight. And so Saint Peter sent forth another little angel. Softly singing he went, winging his way to the earth. Saint Peter watched and waited while guarding his golden gate. Soon this little angel was also lost to sight. Saint Peter wondered where he had wandered, and soon he sent another angel and then another—down to the earth.

The long day passed and not one angel returned. Then the whole host of Heaven's angels hastened to the search. Saint Peter stood at the golden gate, gazing at the movements of the angels over the mountains, the moorlands and meadows, over the valleys and rivers and vast plains of the green earth.

Soon night would fall and the keys of Heaven were not yet found. And so, Saint Peter summoned the archangels and he said, "The golden keys to Heaven's golden gate may have fallen among green plants. Search where golden flowers are blooming. The golden keys may appear as golden yellow blossoms."

Swiftly descended the archangels, first searching among the yellow dead nettles, which since that time have been called "archangels." They searched among the buttercups, the celandine, the coltsfoot, the dandelion, and all yellow flowering plants. But nowhere were the keys to be found.

At last, as night was falling, the first little angel was found, lying fast asleep on the grass. As the archangels gently lifted the sleeping angel to carry him back to Heaven, there beneath him among rough green leaves lay the golden keys.

And from that time on God decreed that this rough-leaved plant should bear blossoms like little bunches of golden keys and should be called "keys of Heaven." That is the old name for cowslips, or paigles, and some people still call them by that name.

Lady's Smock and Marsh Marigolds

Long, long ago, after the three kings had come to visit the Jesus Child, an angel appeared to them and bade them not to return to Herod's court, for cunning Herod had planned to kill the Jesus child. The angel also appeared to Joseph and bade him arise and take Mary and the young child to Egypt until it should be safe to return.

Long and weary was the way to Egypt. The country was dry and dusty without a well or a spring of water.

Day after day, hungry and thirsty they traveled, sleeping by night in caves or under the stars. They longed for water to drink and to wash their clothes. At last they left the dry and dusty desert and came to a kindlier land.

Their little donkey pricked up his ears and trotted to a patch of bright green grass beside a stream of fresh flowing water. He quickly began to crop the grass. Mary filled the golden cup King Melchior had brought to the Jesus Child and they each drank a deep draught of the wonderful cool water.

With the water, Mary washed Jesus's clothes and her own pale lilac smock. After resting by the refreshing waters, Mary blessed the stream and the green, mossy ground that had helped them on their way. As Mary lifted the Jesus Child from where he lay on the soft moss, beside the king's golden cup there blossomed golden flower cups. And on the soft-mossed earth where Mary had spread her lilac smock, delicate mauve flowers appeared.

These flowers, mauve as Mary's smock, we call our lady's smock, and the yellow flowers that grow by the water are called kingcups or marsh marigolds.

Snowdrops

After Adam and Eve were driven out of Paradise, their life was filled with labor. Long were the days, dark were the nights, blazing were the summers, bitter were the winters through which they toiled upon the earth.

One chill winter's day, when the earth was draped in a blanket of snow, Eve remembered the beauty of Paradise, and she was filled with a great longing to glimpse once more the glorious garden she had lost.

Long was the journey she made to the garden, wading through the drifts of the winter's snow. At last, when she reached Paradise, Eve saw cherubim whirling their flaming swords, guarding the gate of the garden.

She gazed through the gate and could glimpse the green grass, the flowering trees, and the ripe, red, fruit. Outside all lay frozen and forlorn, but within the garden all was warm and lush and full with life.

The cherubim were filled with pity for Eve's plight and wished to lighten her pain. So they gathered soft snowflakes in their hands and gently drew near to Eve, giving her these gifts to take back to Earth.

And so she set out on her long wandering. Not long had she traveled before the soft snowflakes began melting in her warm grateful hands, and behold, the snowflakes were little white flower bells.

Rejoicing, Eve planted the flowers in her garden on earth, and every year when the earth seems frozen and forlorn the little snowdrops blossom, ringing like bells, singing songs of Paradise.

The Daisies

It was the Jesus Child's third birthday. Mother Mary wished to make a crown of flowers, but it was winter and there were no flowers to be found, so she took some white linen and some snippets of golden silk, and with great care she cut white petals and arrayed them around a golden center. When she was sewing the last white petals onto the golden center, she pricked her finger and the white petals were flecked with red.

The Jesus Child loved these flowers. When springtime came, he planted them in the earth and blew his breath upon them. He watered them from the golden cup of the kings, and they grew and spread and bloomed all the year round. We call this round flower the day's eye, or daisy, for as the sun sinks to rest, so the daisy's white petals close over the golden center and open again in the morning at sunrise.

The Poplar and the Holly

Long ago, when Joseph and Mother Mary and the Jesus Child were fleeing to Egypt, they heard the sound of galloping horses and the shouts of Herod's soldiers:

"There they are, there they are! We will seize them and bring them to Herod our King!"

Mother Mary, hearing the galloping horses, spoke to a tall poplar tree, hoping that her broad, sweeping branches would protect the holy family. But the tree feared harm to herself, and lest the cruel soldiers should cut her down, shivering and shaking, she lifted her branches to the sky to show the soldiers that no one was hiding beneath them.

Near this fearful tree stood a soft green bush with white berries.

"Come quickly to me. I shall shelter you as best I can," the bush called. And the soft green bush protected the holy family with her branches.

While Herod's men came closer and closer, the brave little bush gathered her strength and grew bigger and bigger. Her soft green leaves grew hard and from them sharp pointed prickles sprouted like spears.

The soldiers saw a glimpse of red—of Mother Mary's dress—in the bush. They reached with their hands into the bush to seize the babe, but their skin was pierced by the sharp prickles, and they could not reach through.

"Those are but berries. No one could hide in such a prickly bush. They have escaped," their commander called. "Mount and come away and ride in pursuit!" And away they rode.

And to this day, holy bush or holly, as we now call it, is sometimes a tall tree with hard leaves that brandish sharp prickles and berries, deep red like Mother Mary's dress, reminding us of how the brave holly once sheltered the holy family.

And the tall, terrified tree that I told you of is called the poplar, which to this day still shivers and shakes and stands rooted like a tower, lifting its head to the clouds, longing for the day when it can again lower its branches and caress the dark earth.

Moss

One day Mary and Jesus were walking together by Nazareth, where the abundant flowers bloom so beautifully in the spring. They wandered on and on, silently listening to the songs of the singing birds, watching the bees and butterflies hovering over a mantle of flowers draping the fields and the hillside.

On their homeward journey, Mary felt weary and wished to rest for a while, but the meadow was full with flowers. Mother Mary was loathe to crush them.

At last, Jesus discovered a soft, green, cushiony plant crowned with starry blossoms. Gently he picked every flower. Then he led his mother to rest on the soft green cushion. The plant was so happy to give Mary such pleasure that from that time on the moss—for that is the name of this soft green plant— only bears little blossoms that one can hardly see. But it spreads its soft green cushion on the ground, making it velvety and most wonderful to rest upon.

The Convolvulus or Bindweed

Long ago, a weary wagoner was endeavoring to free his cart from out of a deep rut into which it had rolled. He gathered his strength and heaved the cart. From side to side it swayed. But alas, it was loaded with big barrels of wine and refused to roll out of the rut. The wagoner sighed, "Stuck fast it is, and stuck fast it will be!"

It so happened that while the wagoner was swaying the cart from side to side, the Mother of God passed by, and seeing the wagoner's plight, she said to the poor man,

"I am tired and thirsty from my travels. Please give me a glass of wine."

The weary wagoner said, "Fain would I give you wine, but I have no glass wherein I could give it you."

Then the Mother of God picked a little white flower cup, which we call bindweed. She gave it to the wagoner, who filled it with wine, and the Mother of God drank the wine.

At once the cart was freed, and the wagoner, with great joy, drove out of the ditch. One could hear the barrels rumble as the wagon rolled out of the rut and raced down the road.

Ever since that day this little flower cup has had pink stripes on its petals from the red wine that the Mother of God drank, and it is called Mary's glass.

The Ragweed

Verses by William Allingham

Long ago the yellow-flowered ragweed had another name. This is how the old name was lost and a new name gained.

One day Tom went out walking, and as he rambled through the fields he heard a sound in a bush nearby. It could have been the wind making that sound, or it could have been a rabbit scurrying down its hole. But the wind makes a softer sound, and a rabbit makes a sharper sound. So he bent down by the bush to see. There he saw a little old man about the size of his thumb. The leprechaun was cobbling a boot and singing this song as he worked:

> "Tip-tap, rip-rap,
> Tick-a-tack-a-too!
> Scarlet leather, sewn together,
> This will make a shoe.
> Left, right, pull it tight;
> Summer days are warm;
> Underground in winter,
> Laughing at the storm!"

Now Tom saw that he might find the crock of gold that all leprechauns have hidden away, if only he could catch the little man and hold him fast until he showed him where to find the treasure.

Carefully Tom crept to the bush. Quickly he grasped the leprechaun in his hand. Leprechauns are very clever, so Tom was determined not to be tricked. Keeping his eyes on his captive, Tom said, "Kindly tell me, little man, where your gold is hid."

"Look behind you!" said the leprechaun. "The cows are in your field and are eating up the oats!"

Tom was so startled that he almost turned to look, but he remembered that he must not take his eyes off the leprechaun. Again he asked, "Kindly tell me, little man, where your gold is hid."

"Look, look!" cried the leprechaun. "There goes your gray mare. She's running away down the road."

Tom was not to be tricked a second time. Holding the leprechaun all the tighter, he said, "Leprechaun, you must show me where the gold is hid before I set you free."

At that, the leprechaun saw that he was caught indeed. He guided Tom to the middle of a large field in which grew many stiff yellow daisy flowers. Pointing to one of these plants, the leprechaun said, "Dig underneath that and you will find the crock of gold."

Tom very cleverly tied the bit of rag that was his garter around the stiff stem of the plant to mark the hidden treasure. And without stopping to thank the leprechaun he ran home to fetch a spade.

Tom ran all the way back too, but when he saw the field he knew that he had been outwitted. For he found that each and every stiff yellow daisy plant had a rag tied around it! Far off he heard the leprechaun singing:

"Tip-tap, rip-rap,
Tick-a-tack-a-too!
Scarlet leather, sewn together,
This will make a shoe.
Left, right, pull it tight;
Summer days are warm;
Underground in winter,
Laughing at the storm!"

And that is how the ragweed got its name.

The Nightingale

Long, long ago there lived a little brown bird that could not sing. All the other birds of the forest sang beautiful melodies, and he listened to them singing and singing all day long, wishing that he too could sing.

One dark night, the poor little bird was perched at the top of a tall, tall tree. His sleepy eyes were closed, his head was warm beneath his wing. Suddenly the whole forest was filled with light, brighter than sunlight, brighter than starlight! All was quiet; no sound was heard, not even a rustling leaf. The little bird held his breath. Then the heavens and the earth resounded with all the heavenly host! Angels filled the air with music and song, praising and glorifying God the Father. As the angels sang, the bird opened his own little beak and began to sing with them, a melody beautiful and clear!

As he sang, he saw far, far away shepherds striding along. He flew and he flew as fast as he could and followed them until they came to a stable where Mother Mary had laid the Jesus Child in a crib. The little bird wished to sing his song to all the world of the sight he saw; but when he tried to sing, there was no song! Only squeaky squawks came out of his open beak.

"Alas and alack! I can no longer sing," he thought. "But I can perch on the crib to keep watch over the child so that no harm shall come to him."

In the night the babe awoke and was restless. He began to cry and cry. So softly the little bird began to sing a beautiful lullaby; the song soothed the child and he fell fast asleep.

Filled with joy, the bird flew out into the night and sang and sang until all the birds in Bethlehem awoke and listened to the song of the nightingale! And even now, in the summer season he sings sometimes in the day, sometimes at night, "Glory to God in the highest and on earth, peace, to men of good will."

How the Robin Got His Red Breast

Long, long ago on the first Christmas, all the world lay sleeping in a deep winter night.

While all the world lay dark and still, a small brown bird slept. A small brown bird curled in his nest; his small brown head beneath his wing.

Suddenly from out of the darkness there shone a great light. Out of the silence came a glorious song. The angels were singing of the Jesus Child's birth. The bird awoke; he opened his bright eyes; he opened his brown wings. Up, up, high in the night sky he flew, high and far he flew till he found where Mary, Joseph, and the Jesus Child lay.

The holy family lay sleeping together quietly. The light of a fire glimmered in the dark. But the flames were sinking low. Soon the warmth would die away and the child would wake with cold. The brown bird flew near, fanning the fire with his soft wings. Bravely he beat until the flames burnt strong and warm and bright. Fierce sparks blazed up and scorched his breast. Yet he only thought of keeping the Jesus Child safe and warm. Still the child slept, but Mother Mary awoke and saw the little bird so small and brown and brave. Mary spoke, "Little bird, I name you robin redbreast. May the radiance of the fire shine forever in your feathers."

So to this day, the robin wears his red breast so that we may remember his courageous heart.

The Easter Hare
W. M. von Heider

In the days when the Jesus Child lived among men, the earth was beginning to die. The stout oaks could no longer withstand the storm, the delicate aspens shook as though with an ague, and the flowers opened their blossoms only to gaze on the sun and wither away. Men and women wandered over the earth with sad hearts and listless eyes.

Only the Jesus Child knew that the world would not die, for he had come to bring life and hope.

So he called the animals to him and said, "Which of you will be my messenger and journey through the world saying to everyone you meet, 'The earth will live anew for the Christ has come'?" Then all the animals pressed around him saying, "Send me, send me." The Jesus Child saw that it would be difficult to choose, so he said, "The one who can most quickly circle the earth and return shall be my messenger."

Then the wild stag thought, "I am the fleetest of foot; I shall win the race." And he went bounding over the hills. But when he came to the rocky highlands he could not resist leaping over crag and burn, and so happy was he in his game that he forgot the passing of the hours.

The salmon said to himself, "I can dart through the water and float with the tide; I shall far outstrip the heavy-footed beasts." But when he saw the sunbeams sparkling on the stream he thought they were golden flies. All day long he leapt, hoping to catch the bright-winged vagrants. And so the day turned to its close.

The hawk exulted, "I am the swiftest of all who circle the earth." And he shot like an arrow through the blue. But suddenly his keen eye saw a tiny field mouse creeping among the corn, straight as a plummet he swooped. His journey was forgotten in the joy of the chase.

Only the hare kept quickly on his way. Turning neither to the right nor the left, gazing ever more

before him, he steadfastly held his course, and just as the sun was setting he completer
earth. Thus it was that the hare became the messenger of Jesus.

But when our Lord told him to bear the good tidings to all mankind, the hare w
fear. "How shall I make them believe me?" he asked. Then the Jesus Child asked the crow
of her eggs. "Show them this egg," said our Lord, "and say, 'Just as the golden yolk shines
child who has come from Heaven has brought the light of the sun to earth. And the earth will not die but
will live anew.'" Then the hare set forth upon his way with joy.

For many years the hare journeyed from place to place telling the glad news, and at last he came
back to the hills of Palestine. But when he returned, he found that Christ had died upon the cross. Cruel
men had brought about his death. His body had been laid in the dark earth. But the hare knew the truth. He
knew that the being of Christ had entered the underworld, and, just as the golden yolk is hidden within the
egg, so the light of Heaven is now to be found in the innermost heart of the earth.

So it is that every spring the hare is still the messenger of joy and brings us the Easter egg as a symbol
of Christ.

Why the Spider Has a Cross

Long ago Joseph, Mother Mary, and the Jesus Child were fleeing to Egypt for safety. The sun scorched them
as they wandered through the dry and dusty desert. Nowhere was a well or water to be found.

Stamp, stamp, stamp, stamp, stamp, stamp, sounded footsteps in the distance. King Herod's soldiers
were coming.

Where could the Holy Family hide?

They gazed to the east, and all they saw was the dry and dusty ground. They gazed to the west, but
nowhere was a haven to be found. They gazed to the south, they gazed all around. But in the north there
was a cave.

Swiftly Joseph led the holy family into the cave; surely here they would be safe from Herod's
soldiers. They were all weary from their travels, and soon they fell asleep.

While they slept a little spindly-legged spider, crouching in the corner of the cave, saw Herod's
soldiers swiftly approaching. He thought, "Surely the holy family will here be found. I must save them. But
I am so frail and weak; whatever can I do? I can spin, I can spin! I will spin a web of silk across the cave."

And while the stamp, stamp, stamp, stamp, stamp, stamp of Herod's soldiers drew nearer, the little
spindly-legged spider patiently wove his silken web across the cave's mouth, and when it was finished he
sprayed it with little blobs of gum.

Even the desert wind had pity and whirled sand against the little web.

When Herod's soldiers neared the cave they saw the spun woven web covered with sand. It looked
old, so old.

"No one is in the cave," cried the captain. "The web is old and unbroken. We must search elsewhere.
Away, away!"

When the holy family awoke, well-rested from their long sleep, Joseph saw the sand-sprayed woven
web at the mouth of the cave. Looking down, he saw the spindly-legged spider standing delicately upon a
rock. Then he knew how the little spider had saved them. And Mother Mary blessed the spider. And to this
day the little spider proudly bears a cross on his back, reminding us of his brave deed.

The Glowworm

Long, long ago there lived a little creature in a dark cave. He was not a caterpillar; nor was he a worm. He was more like a beetle, for he had wings and could fly. One dark and cold winter's day, two travelers passed by the mouth of the cave. The woman rode on an ass, and the old man led an ox. They came into the cave to seek shelter from the bitter winter wind and swirling snow. But in the cave it was dark and cold.

The little creature watched, cowering in his corner, and then he slowly crept from his corner and left the cave.

He thought to himself, "At least I must find some light for these poor people."

As he gazed through the darkness he saw light shining from the sparkling stars, and he started to ascend to the heavens, to bring back some light to shine in the cold, dark cave.

So he flew and he flew and he flew toward the stars. When his tiny wings grew tired, he remembered the woman in the cold cave and he gathered new strength.

And again, he flew and he flew and he flew, but alas, he grew weary, so weary that he nearly fell down, down, down to the dark earth below. But again he remembered the woman in the cold cave, and he gathered new strength and flew on until he reached the stars.

At last, when he reached the stars, he spoke these words: "Far below in the world of men there sits in a dark cave a woman to whom a babe is about to be born. O Lord of the stars, lend me some light to illumine this cave, the home of new life!"

And the Lord of the stars gave the creature a little spark of light and fixed it upon his tail. He joyously thanked them; then down, down, down he flew back to earth.

When he reached the cave, behold, it was flooded with light, radiant as if the sun had come to dwell upon the earth. Mother Mary sat, folding the new born babe in her arms.

Sadly the weary traveler thought, "Of what worth is my little spark of light, now that the cave glows like the sun?" and he crept into his corner of the cave and tried to hide his tiny starry spark.

But Mother Mary saw him and beckoned to him. "Come here to me," she called. "In the darkest night my son brought the light of Heaven to earth. Henceforth your light shall shine at midsummer to remind us of his birth."

We, each and every one,
Will take a ray
Of the midsummer sun
Into the darkness
Of the winter night,
That there be light on earth
For the Christ Child's birth.*

---

*W.M. von Heider

The Turnip*

from Russia

Once upon a time there lived a little old man, a little old woman, their granddaughter, a dog, a cat, and a little mouse. And they all lived together in the same little house.

One day in spring the little old man took a turnip seed and planted it in the earth. The little old man tended it. The sun shone and shone on it. The rain watered and watered it. The wind blew and blew over it. And it grew and it grew and it grew until it had grown to be a very big turnip.

One day in fall the little old man said to the little old woman, "Put some water in the pot and place the pot in the oven and mind it's the biggest pot, for I'm going to pull up the turnip and we'll all have turnip soup for supper."

So the little old woman took the biggest pot and half-filled it with water and placed it in the oven.

The little old man went into the field and caught hold of the turnip and he pulled and he pulled, but he could not pull out that turnip. So the little old man called to the little old woman. She came running and caught hold of the little old man, and they pulled and they pulled, but they could not pull out that turnip. So they called to the granddaughter. She came running and caught hold of the little old woman, and they pulled and they pulled, but they could not pull out that turnip. So they called to the dog. And he came running and caught hold of the granddaughter, and they pulled and they pulled, but they could not pull out that turnip. So they called to the cat. She came running and caught hold of the dog, and they pulled and they pulled, but they could not pull out that turnip. So they called to the little mouse. She came running and caught hold of the cat, and they pulled and they pulled, but they could not pull out that turnip.

Just then a family of beetles came scurrying past so they called to father beetle. He came running and caught hold of the little mouse, and they pulled and they pulled and they pulled, but they could not pull out that turnip. So they called to mother beetle. She came running and caught hold of father beetle, and they pulled and they pulled, but they could not pull out that turnip. So they called to baby beetle. She came scuttling and caught hold of mother beetle, and they pulled and they pulled and they pulled, and *out* came that turnip.

So they all had turnip soup for supper.

---

*This is a good story for practicing nouns, verbs, prepositions, conjunctions, and head and foot positions. It could also be performed by older children.

Plays

The Gifts

Cast of Characters

Mary	Sun
Moon	Star
Lamb	Flower
Stone	Child

MARY: Sun, sun, glorious one,
Have you a gift for my little son?

SUN: Take gold from me, Mother Mary.

MARY: Moon, moon, shining one,
Have you a gift for my little son?

MOON: Take silver from me, Mother Mary.

MARY: Star, star, glimmering one,
Have you a gift for my little son?

STAR: Take shimmer from me, Mother Mary.

MARY: Lamb, lamb, gentle one,
Have you a gift for my little son?

LAMB: Take wool from me, Mother Mary.

MARY: Flower, flower, fragrant one,
Have you a gift for my little son?

FLOWER: Take fragrance from me, Mother Mary.

MARY: Stone, stone, sleeping one,
Have you a gift for my little son?

STONE: Take strength from me, Mother Mary.

MARY: Child, child of Heaven and earth,
Have you a gift for my little son's birth?

CHILD: Take all my love, Mother Mary.

Candles

W. M. von Heider

Cast of Characters

Gnomes	Trees and Flowers
Bees	Children
Angels	Mary

GNOMES: We are the good brown earth;
We are the rocks and the stones
And the cracks filled with soil,
Of the good brown earth.

TREES AND FLOWERS: We are the flowers and the trees
That root deep in the soil
'Twixt the cracks in the rocks
And the stones,
Of the good brown earth.

BEES: We are the bees
That make honey and wax,
From the flowers and the trees
That root deep in the soil
'Twixt the cracks in the rocks
And the stones,
Of the good brown earth.

CHILDREN: We are the children
Who have made the candles,
The gift of the bees
That gather honey and wax
From the flowers and the trees
That root deep in the soil
'Twixt the cracks in the rocks
And the stones,
Of the good brown earth.

ANGELS: We are the angels, the heavenly ones,
Messengers of the stars, moon and sun.
Open your hearts, and take our light
To kindle the candles
In the holy night.

The gift of the children,
The gift of the bees
That make honey and wax
From the flowers and the trees
That root deep in the soil
'Twixt the cracks in the rocks
And the stones,
Of the good brown earth.

MARY: I am Mary, the mother meek and mild,
Mary, the mother of the Holy Child.
I take your gifts with gratitude;
Gifts of Heaven and earth you bring
For the birth of the heavenly, earthly king,
The light of the world.

ALL: On his birthday tree in the holy night,
The light of angels in the hearts of men
Shall kindle the candles,
The gift of the children,
The gift of the bees,
The gift of the flowers and the trees,
The gifts of the good brown earth.
    Heaven and earth unite
    In the light
    Of the Christmas tree.

The Winter King

Eileen Hutchins

Cast of Characters

Children	**Salamanders**
Gnomes	**Mary**
Undines	**Joseph**
Sylphs	**Angels**

CHILDREN: We go to seek the winter king,
And as we go we gaily sing;
Through wind and rain, through ice and snow,
With joyous courage let us go.

GNOMES: Hack, hack,
The rocks we crack!
Quake, quake,
The mountains shake.
Bang, bang!
Our hammers clang.
In caverns old
We seek for gold,
And crystals bright
We bring to light.

CHILDREN: O gnomes so wise,
You surely know
All secrets that
The earth can show;
Tell us the way
We have to go
To find the king
Of ice and snow.

GNOMES: We do not know,
We cannot tell,
Which way you go,
So fare you well,
But take this gift,
A crystal bright,
Unto our king
This winter's night.

Song

UNDINES: Over the waters
            And over the waves,
            Floating in foam
            Through the ocean caves;
            Drifting in mist
            On the lonely shore,
            Homeless we wander
            For evermore.

CHILDREN: O Undines all,
            You surely know
            All realms through which
            Your rivers flow.
            Tell us the way,
            We humbly crave,
            To find the king
            Of the ocean wave.

UNDINES: We do not know,
            We cannot tell,
            Which way you go,
            So fare you well,
            But take this
            Waterlily white,
            Unto our king
            This winter's night.

Song

SYLPHS: As we fly, as we fly,
            On the wings of the light,
            With the clouds through the sky,
            With the wind in its flight;
            All the birds in their winging
            Will follow our way,
            As they greet with their singing
            The light and the day.

CHILDREN: O Sylphs! O Sylphs!
            You surely know
            All realms through which
            Your breezes blow.
            Tell us the way
            We have to fare
            To find our king
            Of mist and air.

SYLPHS: We do not know,
We cannot tell,
Which way you go,
So fare you well,
But take this gift,
A feather white,
Unto our king
This winter's night.

Song

SALAMANDERS: Burning brightly,
Flaming fiercely,
Soaring heavenward
Leaps the fire.
We flash and we flame,
We scorch and we sear,
Beware of our fire
And come not near.

CHILDREN: O Salamanders,
You surely know
The light of Heaven
Where starfires glow.
Tell us the way
This frosty night,
Where we may find
The king of light.

SALAMANDERS: We do not know,
We cannot tell,
Which way you go,
So fare you well,
But take this gift,
A flaming light,
Unto our king
This winter's night.

(Song follows.)

Song

We go to seek the win-ter king, And as we go we gai- ly sing, Through wind and rain, through ice and snow, With joy- ous cou-rage le _____ t us go _____.

(The children come to the crib, they kneel and give their gifts to Mother Mary.
Behind Mother Mary and Joseph there are many angels.)

Michaelmas Play
Rosemary Gebert
(to be performed by grades 1, 2, 3, and 4)

Cast of Characters

Gnomes (Grade 1)   **Meteors** (Grade 2)
Dragon (Grade 3)   **Men and Women** (Grade 4)
Voice of Saint Michael (in eurythmy)   **King**

MEN AND WOMEN:
Fierce is the dragon's might,
Desperate is our plight,
All are dismayed.

KING:
We who on earth must dwell
Call on Saint Michael
To lend us his aid!

VOICE OF SAINT MICHAEL:
Sparks from my sword I send;
Swift be the dragon's end.

METEORS:
Bright-gliding meteors
Curve through the night.
Michael's messengers,
Silent our flight.

(They run across scattering stars they have made themselves.)

MEN AND WOMEN:
See now, Saint Michael
Answers our call.
Catch the bright falling stars
Quick as they fall!
Forge their bright metal
To breastplate and shield,
To heaven-sent weapons
The dragon shall yield!

(They collect stars and give them to the gnomes.)

GNOMES:
We will work
With a will,
With our strength,

anapest

With our skill,
With a clash,
And a clang,
On our anvils we'll bang
Till the armor shines bright!

(Gnomes give weapons to men.)

MEN: Now we are guarded well,
Head, heart, and hand.
We'll drive the dragon forth
Out of our land.

(Exit men.)

ALL SING: "In autumn, Saint Michael" *(see p. 92)*

GNOMES: Help from on high men sought,
Magic the stars they caught,
Wisdom of ancient days
Lives in the swords we wrought.

WOMEN: Gnomes, we thank you from our hearts.

(Re-enter men.)

MEN: Listen while we tell our story:
Michael in all his glory
Fought beside us in the field,
Helped us make the dragon yield.
The monster lies upon the ground,
In iron bands he's safely bound.

(Enter Grade 3 in a long line holding on to each other, their heads bent. The first child wears a dragon's head; the other children are covered by a painted cloth. They are led in and then they kneel down.)

ALL: Tamed now shall the monster be,
And we from wicked spells are free!

WOMEN: So for joy let's dance and sing,

Fast and faster, round the ring,
This way, that way, leap and spring!

(Singing and dancing.)

MEN AND WOMEN:	Where he fell We'll build a mill, To grind our corn We'll bend his will, His strength shall serve Our land to till. And we shall never let him go, Until he's learnt to serve us so.
ALL:	Give thanks to Michael, Christ's right hand, Who gave us strength to free our land. To good the dragon's will we'll bend And so redeem him in the end.
ALL SING:	"O strong unconquered knight of God."

Chapter Three

Grade Three (Ages Eight to Nine)

The main lesson subjects for this year are farming, housebuilding, Old Testament stories, grammar, and weights and measures.

Why do children approaching this age often want to run away to see the world? Why does everything have to be "fair"? "It's not fair" is a new vocabulary that creeps in at this time.

Why do they often begin to doubt that Mummy is really their own Mummy? Why do they suddenly want their own gardens, however small? Why are they no longer content to work alongside their mothers or fathers? Why do they get headaches or feel sick, genuinely, on certain days at certain times? Why are there days and times when they can no longer quite cope with certain lessons? Why do children who have hitherto been quiet, happy, and obedient often become critical and awkward? Why do some begin to show off and grow belligerent, while others often become pale and lose their appetite? Why do they love riddles at this age?

The following conversations may help to answer some of these questions.

Child: "How many lives have you got?"
Teacher: "How many have *you* got, Vicky?"
Child: "I've got three. I've got my home life and I've got my school life and then I've got my own life."

One day Saint Nicholas came with his servant, Rupert, to read out of his book. He handed Rupert sweets, nuts, and apples to give to the children. The children were quite overawed, just as they had been in the second grade, but with this difference. No sooner had Saint Nicholas and Rupert closed the classroom door behind them than a violent argument broke out.

"I know who it was. Saint Nicholas was Mr. M."

"No, he wasn't, he was Mr. B."

"I know he was Mr. M. because I could see his shoes."

"Well, I know it was Mr. B. because I could tell by his voice."

Voices rose high, until suddenly a child flung herself between the two sides. She stamped her foot and shouted with tears in her eyes, "I don't care who he was, he was Saint Nicholas to me."

The children began to eat their apples and the argument was forgotten.

A child came skipping into the classroom one morning bubbling over with glee.

"I'm going to be naughty today, I am," she declared.

"Why?" asked her teacher.

"I am, I'm going to be really naughty."

"But why?"

"Because I love you when you're angry."

Unless a child is a happy, healthy country child—and such children are few and far between these days—he or she will need special help and patient understanding in Grades 3 and 4. Until now children have lived at one with the world. Suddenly they become aware of themselves and aware of the world. They begin to see their families and friends from outside. They are overpowered by the greatness of the world, and they are often overpowered by their own smallness and weakness. This can frighten them, it can also make them belligerent. They can feel bitter disappointment and frustration.

When we look at the curriculum for Grade 3, we can see that it meets with the needs of children at this stage.

The Bible stories give them the sense of security for which they long. Moses leads the children of Israel out of Egypt through the wilderness and into the promised land. Jehovah punishes and rewards them; he guides and shelters them; he is a pillar of fire by night and a cloud by day. Children identify with the children of Israel. They ask for justice, punishment, and reward. They want no to mean no, however hard they may kick against it, so that they know how they stand in relationship to the world. They want to be able to trust adults, but when adults give in to them, they mistrust them.

Farming and housebuilding show them that man is not alone in this great world but is here to work with others, with the soil, plants, animals, and seasons, with the sun, moon, and stars.

At the age of nine, children become aware of their own dwelling, in which they are learning to live on earth. It is good for them to listen to the major and minor thirds and to very simple major and minor arpeggios. They do not yet learn the Eurythmy movement for the major and minor thirds; they just listen for the melody to take them into their own house, or into the outside world. Children do not experience minor melodies as sad, but as a necessary going inside.

"My house has an open door to the world so wide

And silver steps to the stars inside."

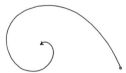

can be used as an introduction

The class teacher and Eurythmy teacher can work together fully at this time, each helping the children to find themselves and discover the world, to breathe freely in and out, to wake well and sleep well. At this time, the exercise of Contraction and Expansion is healing for children. They have, no doubt, often done it before as play, but now they really need it and must work with it. Many are the ways in which it can be practiced in all lessons at this time.

When the Bible stories are told to the children, the Eurythmy lessons could begin with God's promise to Noah.

While the earth remaineth,	**Standing,**
Seedtime	**contraction.**
and	
harvest,	**Expansion,**
Cold	**contraction.**
and	
heat,	**Expansion,**
Summer	**expansion.**
and	
winter,	**Contraction,**
Day	**expansion.**
and	
night	**Contraction,**
Shall not cease.*	**standing.**

Just by moving toward each other and away from each other, the children begin to breathe differently; they need to experience this life rhythm of contraction and expansion very deeply at this time.

Spiral forms, too, should be practiced consciously during this time and could be introduced during housebuilding.

Now is the time to begin the Concentration Exercises. The children cannot copy anyone; they have to rely entirely on themselves; they have to learn to remember and also to think ahead. Children can, of course, do concentration exercises earlier, just as they can learn to read at four and five, but it doesn't do them any good. After nine, they really need these exercises. Rhythms too, which until now they have danced, should be learned and done accurately, not stopping on the long beat, but really moving forward into the stream of the rhythm and experiencing the short beats as pulsating and the long beats as breathing or flowing.

The Concentration Exercises can be built up gradually from the child's ninth birthday and continued right through the school. Endless variations can be invented. Care should be taken that the exercises never become mechanical, and that the children learn to move freely and courageously backward, not hunched or hesitantly. As the pupils grow older they will understand the value of these exercises.

When children are in their ninth year, many things that they did naturally in their early years become foreign to them. They used to become completely absorbed in their drawing, tongues accompanying the movement of the hand. At nine, tongues can't stop talking, words come tumbling out.

They used to be ready for their Eurythmy lessons. When they are nine, the teacher is sometimes confronted with a tangle of arms and legs on the floor. The good habits that the children learned in the preschool and Grades 1 and 2 tend to disappear. Just as Moses had to insist on obedience with the children of Israel, so now the teacher must insist, again and again. The teacher has to insist that tongues are still, hands are clean, hair is tidy, shirts are tucked in, socks are pulled up—thundering at them one minute and speaking very quietly the next, insisting on order and quiet before the lesson begins. It might take fifteen

---

*Genesis, Chapter 8, verse 2.

minutes the first time, ten minutes the next, but the day will surely come when the children will give you the surprise of your life. They will all be spick and span and ready for you. This must be treated like a birthday present. There is no guarantee it will happen again next week. Eventually they will get used to being ready for the Eurythmy lesson; they will know that the time lost at the beginning of a lesson has to be made up in recess or after school.

The children should take turns to be the "leader" or "helper." This week's leader will be the last in the line next week and shut the door. At the end of the lesson, indicate what you will be doing in the next lesson and nominate next week's leader. Remember birthday children and let them choose a special exercise. Thus a link can be made from lesson to lesson.

A September Lesson with Grade 3

This could be planned based on the legend of the dragon of Ireland.

Enter with song, "On the earth I love to stand." *(see page 46)** This could be done in connection with the curve of Cassini which the children should know well by this time.

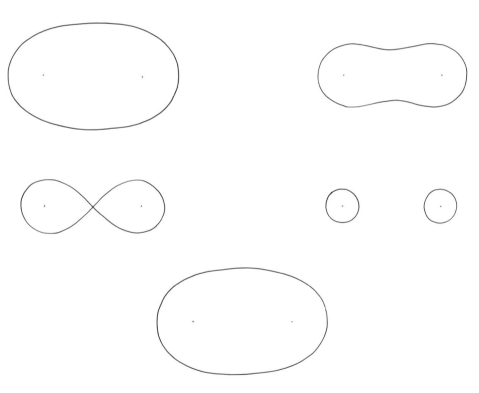

Verse:

Earth is dark and fear is lurking,   **Contraction**
Oh Saint Michael, Heaven's knight,   **expansion**
Go before us now and lead us
Out of darkness into light.   (Contraction and Expansion)

Begin the story and tell how the dragon comes

> Out of the surging sea,
> Slinky and slimy,
> Creeping and crawling,
> Raging and roaring,
> The dragon is here.
>
> See how it opens its yawning jaws,
> Hear how it scrapes its scaly claws.
>
> Are we afraid?
> No! We are brave.
>
> Brave and true I will be,
> Each good deed sets me free.
> Each kind thought makes me strong.
> I will fight for the right,
> I will conquer the wrong.
>
> I will conquer the wrong,
> I will fight for the right.
> Each kind thought makes me strong,
> Each good deed sets me free.
> Brave and true I will be.

This is an energetic anapest and should be done with precision. The children should move rhythmically forward and then repeat the lines in reverse order, stepping it backward.

The king of Ireland's knights must learn to take one step and stop still, standing firm and unshakeable as a rock. Then they take two steps and stand firm as a rock, three steps, and so on, getting faster and faster up to seven steps. Then they run seven steps backward and stop, six steps, and so on, getting slower and slower. The knights can also take one step forward and stop, then two steps backward, fearlessly, and stop, three steps forward, and so on. Then they take their shining swords and step the iambic rhythm of the song.

German Folksong

> O strong unconquered knight of God,
>   Saint Michael,
> In battle wield with us thy sword,
> Help us below, to fight the foe,
>   Saint Michael!
>
> Thou bearest Heaven's banner free,
>   Saint Michael!

Iambic rhythm beginning with left foot on short beat and holding the middle of the rod in the right hand and stretching straight in front so that the rod is vertical on the long beat.

Thy kingly legions angels be,
Help us below to fight the foe,
    Saint Michael!

Strong may thy valiant armies be,
    Saint Michael!
Strong on land and strong on sea,
Help us below to fight the foe,
    Saint Michael!

Although all the knights of Ireland practiced in order to become strong and skilful, not one alone was strong enough to kill the dragon who by now had devoured all the cattle and had ringed around the town with his scaly body. All the people of the city together could surely kill him. They made a great circle and began to march outward to where the monster lay, but their courage failed them and they turned their backs on him and said to each other:

I'm so weak	Standing,
And so are you,	contraction,
What shall we do?	four steps to center
What shall we do?	of circle.
Courage and strength	Standing,
Are glowing in me;	beginning to expand,
I'll turn and face the enemy.	turn out,
Fear is fled and I am free.	run and jump to periphery.

The people of Ireland hurled their spears, but the dragon did not move. His stillness was frightening. Again they felt helpless and turned toward each other saying:

I'm so weak
And so are you,
What shall we do?
What shall we do?

Courage and strength
Are glowing in me;
I'll turn and face the enemy.
Fear is fled and I am free.

Again, they hurled their swords, hayforks, and knives at the dragon. He still did not move. They drew nearer and saw he was already dead—killed by the sword of Saint Michael, who, when we gather strength to fight, goes before us and slays the dragon.

The Dragon of Ireland

In the middle of the tenth century, when King Elgar ruled over Ireland and Ivor, the archbishop of Norwegian ancestry, had his seat at Armagh, the country was beset with great trouble. A dragon, which surely the jaws of hell had brought forth, spread destruction over the entire island. The creature was horrible to behold. Its body was stronger than that of the most powerful lizard from the primeval forest of Simerick, and its scales, which formed an invincible coat of mail, glittered uncannily, now in emerald green, now in fiery red. As for the head, bloodthirsty eyes flashed forth under the sharp horns, and the monstrous mouth with its three layers of teeth and fangs spewed forth deadly poison.

Nothing could hinder its advance, not the mountains of basalt with their steep precipices, not the rushing rivers, not even the bay of the ocean with its heaving, crashing waves. Wherever the monster went, it left ruins in its wake. The fields over which its heavy body took its course remained forever barren, and if it happened to pass through wheat fields in order to attack horses and cattle by surprise it was as if a firebrand had singed all the grass. The waters of the rivers from which it drank stank thereafter, and the forests into which it withdrew for the night were filled with pestilence and poisoned the land.

For some time the dragon satisfied itself by devouring animals, then it began to creep around the city after dark and seize upon those people who had stayed out too late. Women passing along the beach with their washing and children returning home fell victim by the hundreds. No one dared go out anymore, neither in rich cities nor in poor villages, and men commended their souls to God.

At long last, after the king had gone to the archbishop for advice, it was decided to declare war on the monster. Ivor, the bishop, ordered a strict three-day fast. After the bravest soldiers in Armagh had assembled, the attack was set for the day of the festival of Saint Patrick. The dragon had its lair a mile from the city, on desolate heathland, far from the forests. This was a favorable place for a battle, and it was decided to surround the dragon from all sides.

Early in the morning the warriors approached, armed with spears, swords, and poisonous arrows. In front of them under the waves of the cross and banner the relics of holy Ireland were carried in a precious casket. Yet in spite of their piety, all trembled as they went forward. There was the monster! What discord arose among all the warriors! Should they call the attack, or was it better to flee? But soon their faith in God returned and with a fearful shout they flung their spears and lances at the monster. The monster lay without moving as though he slept—or was he already dead? The bravest of the crowd went up to the dragon and made ready to stab it with a sword. But—oh, wonder—it was really dead, and from a tiny wound that was not made by any Irish weapon, from which a stream of black blood flowed. Thereupon the people fell upon the corpse and hacked it to pieces. Then they fetched twigs and dried grass, and lit a fire. Soon nothing was left of the monster but a pile of ashes.

Then the archbishop discovered under the embers a shield and a sword, which surely could not have been used in war. They looked as dainty as a child's toy—a round shield of cedar wood with hard leather straps, golden buckles, and amethyst and topaz; and a sword of the finest steel with a delicate hilt, whose point still showed traces of the blood of the monster. The archbishop knelt down before the weapons, lifted them high, and they were brought in a triumphant procession to the cathedral of Armagh, where the crowd sang the Te Deum.

One thing was certain: God had wrought a miracle in the holy island. Yet who was the heavenly messenger who with such tiny weapons had slain the monster? When the archbishop had gone to sleep after long prayer, the Archangel Michael appeared to him and ordered him to bring the weapons without delay to his favorite sanctuary on earth. But before the archbishop could ask the leader of the heavenly hosts the name of this place, Michael had vanished. Thereupon the archbishop chose two priests to carry the weapons and, with the help of God, discover the place the archangel had in mind. Over the sea to England they steered, and then they crossed the sea a second time and landed in France, turning their steps toward Italy, because they believed nothing else than that Mount Gargano, where Saint Michael was honoured, was the goal of their journey. So they walked southward, until they noticed that against their will they walked again and again toward the west. In whichever way they set out, the sun went down again and again before their eyes. Therefore it was clear: Mount Gargano was not meant, and they prayed to Saint Michael for guidance, not knowing which way to go, and their feet wounded from the long walk. At one point, they were dead tired, filled with doubts, and fearful of the anger of the Irish people and dismissal by their bishop, and they prayed more fervently than ever to God. Thereupon the Angel Michael appeared to them and spoke, "Turn your steps toward Mount Tumbe. There is my true dwelling."

A pious hermit with whom they spent the night showed them the way, and thirty days later they reached the wave-battered mountain. With beating hearts they knocked on the door of the cloister. The prior himself opened the door to them with the words, "I have awaited you, dear brothers! Last night in a dream, I learned the reason for your pilgrimage and know also whence you come after such a long and weary wandering. Give the glorious weapons unto us and then let us give God laud and thanks."

From this day on the weapons rested in the treasury of the cloister, and for five hundred years they were honored by believing pilgrims. In the year 1580 Arthur de Cose, the Bishop of Contames, whose priest's vows did not keep him from stealing, took the treasure of Mont-Saint-Michel for himself. From then on all the precious trophies of Ireland were lost.

Mother Earth

Eileen Hutchins

Mother Earth,
Mother Earth,
Take our seed
And give it birth.

Father Sun,
Gleam and glow
Until the roots
Begin to grow.

Sister Rain,
Sister Rain,
Shed thy tears
To swell the grain.

Brother Wind,
Breathe and blow
Then the blade
Green will grow.

Earth and sun
And wind and rain,
Turn to gold
The living grain.

Grace

Gladys Hahn

For the dark earth that cradles the seed;
For the rain that brings forth the green leaves;
For the stars that give form to the flowers;
For the warm sun that ripens the fruit;
For all this goodness and beauty,
Oh Heavenly Father, we thank Thee.

Verses for Contraction and Expansion

When Days are Darkest
Pelham Moffat

When days are darkest the earth enshrines	contract circle
The seeds of summer's birth;	expand circle
The spirit of man is a light that shines	expand circle
Deep in the darkness of earth.	contract circle

I Gather All My Strength
Pauline Wehrle

I gather all my strength to fight,
I am prepared with all my might,
But now that I behold my foe
I laugh aloud and home I go.

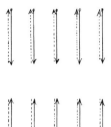

We Are Robbers
Barbara Glas

We are robbers, bold and burly,
Fat and lean and straight and curly.
   Ho! ho! ho! ho!
Fights for us are furious fun,
Lions could not make us run!
   No, no, no, no, no, no, no, no!

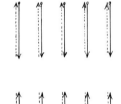

I Think I See an Enemy
Thelma Bowron

I think I see an enemy—
No, he's (she's) my friend.
Ha, ha, ha, ha, ha!

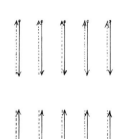

Harvest Song

In autumn Saint Michael with sword and with shield,
Passes over meadow and orchard and field.
He's on the path to battle 'gainst darkness and strife,
He is the heavenly warrior, protector of life.

The harvest let us gather with Michael's aid;
The light he sheddeth fails not, nor does it fade.
And when the corn is cut and the meadows are bare
We'll don Saint Michael's armour and onward will fare.

We are Saint Michael's warriors with strong heart and mind;
We forge our way through darkness Saint Michael to find.
And there he stands in glory; Saint Michael we pray,
Lead us on to battle and show us thy way.

Our Daily Bread

W. M. von Heider

For our daily bread we thank Thee, Father,
We thank the sun and stars and moon;
We thank the wind and frost and rain,
We thank the earth, we thank the grain,
We thank the beasts and all farming men.

God bless the ploughman,
And God bless his team,

As he ploughs, as he ploughs,
As he ploughs the land.

God bless the sower,
And God bless the seed,
As he sows, as he sows,
As he sows the land.

God bless the reaper,
And God bless the scythe,
As he reaps, as he reaps,
As he reaps the corn.

God bless the thresher,
And God bless his flail,
As he threshes, as he threshes,
As he threshes the corn.

God bless the miller,
And God bless his mill,
As he grinds, as he grinds,
As he grinds the corn to flour.

God bless the baker,
And God bless the dough,
As he kneads, as he kneads,
As he bakes it into bread.

God bless the father,
And God bless the mother,
And all the little children too;
As they eat, as they eat,
The bread
And grow strong,
And praise Thee
That they may
Plough, plough, plough;
Sow, sow, sow;
Reap, reap, reap;
Thresh, thresh, thresh;
Grind, grind, grind;
Bake, bake, bake;
And eat their daily bread
For which we thank Thee, Father.

Harvest

Traditional

The boughs do shake and the bells do ring,
So merrily comes our harvest in,
Our harvest in, our harvest in,
So merrily comes our harvest in.

We've ploughed, we've sowed,
We've reaped, we've mowed,
We've got our harvest in.
We've got our harvest in.

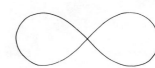

So let us dance and let us sing
Merrily, merrily round the ring.
Our farming year is well begun
We've got our harvest in,

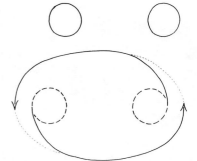

We've got our harvest in, hurrah!

Apple-Howling Song

Old English

Here stands a good apple tree;
Stand fast at root—bear well at top,
Every little twig—bear an apple big,
Every little bough—bear an apple now.
Hats full! Caps full! Three score sacks full!
Hello, boys! Hello!

Blow, Wind, Blow

Traditional

Blow, wind, blow!
And go, mill, go!
That the miller may grind his corn;
That the baker may take it,
And into bread make it,
And bring us a loaf in the morn,
And bring us a loaf in the morn.

The Scarecrow

Traditional

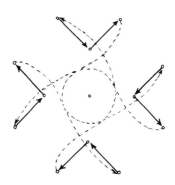

We've ploughed our field,
We've sown our seed,
We've made all neat and gay;
Then take a bit and leave a bit,
Away, birds away.

My Maid Mary

Traditional

My maid Mary,
She minds the dairy,
While I go a-hoeing and mowing each morn;
Merrily runs the reel,
And the little spinning wheel
Whilst I am a-singing and mowing my corn.

Charm for a House and Garden

Cecil Harwood

Spirits of sun and earth and air,
Ye have made this garden fair;
Flower and singing bird and tree,
Ye have blessed all things that be;
For this place be blessing too,
All we think and speak and do,
Beauty here with courage keep,
Banish fear and folly sleep;
Spirits wise and good we rouse,
Love and joy be in this house.

Creation

Old English

This I learnt among men
As the greatest of wonder:
That there was once no earth
Nor the heavens above,
Neither mountain nor tree,
That the sun did not shine,

And the moon gave no light,
Nor was there the sea,
In the depths there was darkness
And the vast spaces were void,
But there was God the Father
Of all beings the mightiest,
And with Him were spirits divine.

God with All-Commanding Might

John Milton

God with all-commanding might
Filled the new-made world with light.
He the golden-tressed sun
Caused all day his course to run,
And the moon to shine by night
With her spangled sisters bright.

Christmas (III)

W. M. von Heider

Behold a babe in Bethlehem
Was born at dead of night.
And all the world was filled with love,
With life and light.

Breton Carol

Traditional

When goodman winter comes again,
    Sing to the earth;
He covers up his blessed grain,
    Sing to the earth.

Sleep quietly, Jean-the-wheat,
    Till spring and winter meet;
Sing to the gentle earth,
    Mother of bread, mother of birth.

Last line standing.

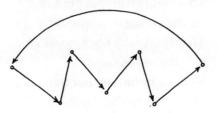

Welsh Folk Song, Suo Gan

Rhythm and spirals

Winter creeps,
Nature sleeps,
Birds are gone,
Fields are bare,
Bleak the air,
Leaves are shed,
All seems dead.

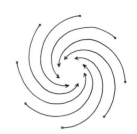

(There are two versions of the second verse.)

But the spring
Soon will bring
Early buds
To the woods;
Lambs will play
All the day;
Naught but green
Will be seen.

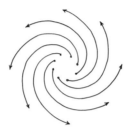

God's alive,
Grow and thrive,
Hidden away
Bloom of May
Rose of June.
Very soon
Naught but green
Will be seen.

One Misty, Moisty Morning

Traditional

One misty, moisty morning,
When cloudy was the weather,
I chanced to meet an old man,
Dressed all in leather,
With his cap right under his chin,
He began to compliment
And I began to grin.
How do you do? How do you do?
How do you do again?

Nimble E (a)

The Sky and the Earth

W. M. von Heider

There's the firm earth under me,
The blue sky over me,
So I stride,
So I stand.
And I see you too,
With the blue sky over you,
The firm earth under you.

Rod exercises in eight—down, up, right, left, right, up, down.

Concentration Exercises

These exercises are intended only for children of the grades indicated or older.

Basic Pattern of the
Exercise in Eight (Grade 3)

1 2 3 4 5 6 7 8	**Skip and clap loudly.**
1 2 3 4 5 6 7 •	**On • stand silently.**
1 2 3 4 5 6 • •	
1 2 3 4 5 • • •	
1 2 3 4 • • • •	
1 2 3 • • • • •	
1 2 • • • • • •	
1 • • • • • • •	
• • • • • • • •	**Stand in silence.**
• • • • • • • 8	
• • • • • • 7 8	
• • • • • 6 7 8	
• • • • 5 6 7 8	
• • • 4 5 6 7 8	
• • 3 4 5 6 7 8	
• 2 3 4 5 6 7 8	
1 2 3 4 5 6 7 8	**Skip and clap loudly.**

Variations:

(a) Skip 8.
    Walk 7, 1 back and clap.
    Walk 6, 2 back and clap.
    Walk 5, 3 back and clap,
    (*And so on until*)
    Skip 8 backward clapping.
    Walk 7 backward clapping, 1 step forward.
    Walk 6 backward clapping, 2 steps forward
    (*And so on until*)
    Last 8 steps forward skipping.

(b) As a *canon* in two groups:
    Second group begins by skipping forward 8 steps when first group is skipping 8 steps backward with clapping.

(c) Partners hold hands and turn in the opposite direction (together); first on 8, then 7 and 8, then 6, 7, and 8, and so on. Skip the whole exercise!

Shepherds' Hey or Three Meet

Music for the basic pattern and the variations of the Concentration Exercise in Eight.

The Walls of Asgard (Turrets and Towers)
Grade 4

Music: Butterflies' Country Dance

Basic Step: 1, 2, 3, across.

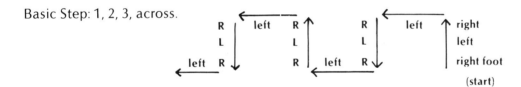

This can be done in two groups starting at opposite ends, or in one group starting alternately. (When the first child has done "1, 2, 3, across," the second child can begin, and so on.)

1, 2, 3, turn,
1, 2, 3, continue
on the other side

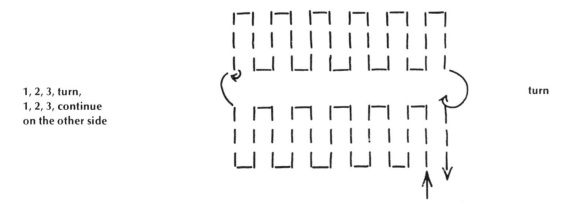

turn

Butterflies' Country Dance

Fine

Exercises in Four (Grade 5)

Either standing or walking backwards on 1 and so on.

<u>1</u> 2 3 4   ♩♩ 0 0 0   <u>1</u> 2 3 4
1 <u>2</u> 3 4   0 ♩♩ 0 0   1 <u>2</u> 3 4
1 2 <u>3</u> 4   *or*   0 0 ♩♩ 0   *or*   1 2 <u>3</u> 4
1 2 3 <u>4</u>   0 0 0 ♩♩   1 2 3 <u>4</u>
<u>1</u> 2 3 4   ♩♩ 0 0 0   1 2 <u>3</u> 4
1 <u>2</u> 3 4   0 ♩♩ 0 0   1 <u>2</u> 3 4
1 2 <u>3</u> 4   0 0 ♩♩ 0   <u>1</u> 2 3 4
1 2 3 <u>4</u>   0 0 0 ♩♩

Flying Exercise (Grade 5)

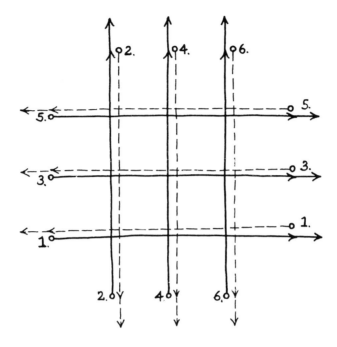

Count 8 steps or 6 according to space available. With arms horizontal, the children leap across with 8 (6) slip-steps to their partner's place. Number ones go first, then number twos, and so on.

Variations:

(a) When number ones are half-way across (count 4), number twos begin on the fifth count, and so on.
(b) Call pairs at random, for example, fours (2, 3, 4); sevens (2, 3, 4); fives (2, 3, 4); ones (2, 3, 4), and so on.

Chapter Four

Grade Four (Ages Nine to Ten)

The main lesson subjects for this year are home surroundings, man and animal, Norse myths, decimals and fractions, and grammar.

All that children experience before their eighth year we can experience in the vowel sound A (à). We can experience children's openness to all worlds, their gradually coming to dwell within their own "houses," and the streaming of the formative forces from the head downward. In the vowel sound A (à), we become again as little children.

All that children experience after the ninth year, we can experience in the vowel sound E (ā). We can experience how they come in from an expansion to a contraction. We can experience their feeling of awakening, their pain, their feeling of danger, their awareness of themselves where their arms cross and the world beyond into which their hands are directed.

A very helpful exercise at this time is *Geschicklichkeit,* E (ā)—skilful or nimble, E (ā). This exercise can be practised by the whole class, either round the classroom or in the Eurythmy lessons. The children walk, doing an energetic E (ā) with their wrists and legs, the one leg crossing the other with the ankle at the side of the knee.

The children must become brave warriors; warriors can endure a hurt without flinching. At the end of the exercise, the children will show the red marks on their wrists with pride. If this exercise is practiced regularly, the children will become more aware of their actions, they will feel secure and steadier in themselves and not lose their belonging so often and so easily.

When the children are nine, the imitative forces are transformed, bringing them into a new relationship with speech. Norse mythology can give children mighty echoing alliterations, with which they can stamp themselves through the consonants and into the world.*

Alliterations can be practiced by groups of children in wedge formation; they can move forward or diagonally. Alliterations can also be practiced in a circle with a child beginning the "running wave" swirling in from the outside and spiraling a consonant around the next child in the circle as he or she stamps forward. That child then takes the consonant on the wave to the next child.

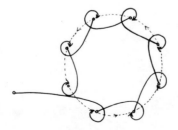

---

*Rudolf Steiner discusses the creative power of the word, and the northern Germanic tribes and their fights with the Romans, in *Karmic Relationships,* vol. 1, lecture 9, Rudolf Steiner Press, London.

An alliteration is one of the few Eurythmy exercises that can be done out of doors. Get a Grade 4 group into fighting formation and march them outside to battle against a strong wind. Let them shout into their shields as they stamp into the storm.

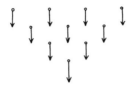

When the children are working with the Norse myths, they can learn to "Build the Walls of Asgard." This is a concentration exercise with many variations. The basic form is like the turrets of a tower. Practice first in a circle; beginning with the right foot, take three steps forward; then with the left foot, take one step across. Then step back three steps. This can also be done as a canon or round. One child begins 1, 2, 3, across, then as he or she steps back, the next child begins forward so that each child is four steps behind the child in front. At the end of the row, the count is 1, 2, 3, turn; 1, 2, 3, across. The turn takes the turret back along the other side of the room and each new opposite number is greeted. (See Chapter Three, the section, "Concentration Exercises.")

During the man and animal main lesson, the children could continue grammar in the Eurythmy lessons. They have already been taught some parts of speech in the Bible stories of Grade 3. Now they can be divided into groups—a group of verbs running, a group of "signpost" words (prepositions) directing, a group of conjunctions linking words and sentences, a group of words describing verbs, a group of words describing nouns, and so on. Each group must be alert, listening for their special part of speech and dovetailing their movement into the whole. In a poem like Tennyson's "The Eagle," the apollonian forms give a picture of the rocky crags, which the children will enjoy drawing as well as moving. It gives the children a tremendous satisfaction to experience the structure of language through Eurythmy.

He clasps the crag with crooked hands

Close to the sun in lonely lands,

Ringed with the azure world, he stands.

Grammar can also be very rousing and engaging if taught in connection with Norse mythology. See the following examples from *The Prose Edda.**

Nouns

In *The Prose Edda,* what are the names of the air and the wind? Air is called Yawning Void, Middle World, Bird Abode, and Wind Abode.

Wind is called, among other names, Storm, Breeze, Gale, Tempest, Gust, and Blowing.

And here are more names for the wind.

> *Wind* 'tis called among menfolk,
> And *Waverer* with the Gods—
> *Neigher* the great powers name it;
> *Shrieker* the giants,
> And *Shouter* the elves call it;
> In hell, *Clamorer* 'tis called.
> The wind is also called *Blast.*†

Verbs

The teacher can ask: "What does the wind *do?*"

The children answer:

> He blows the clouds along.
> He bends the trees.
> He drives the smoke.
> He whips up sand.
> He lashes water into waves.
> He caresses the tiny flowers.
> He whispers among the leaves.
> He sighs among the sedges.
> He whistles around corners and in keyholes.
> He howls in the chimneys.
> He drives the sailing ships along.
> He hums in the telegraph wires,
> He sways high buildings.
> He carries the eagle high in the air.
> He rattles the windows and doors.
> He carries the seeds along.
> He swoops down on people and takes off their hats.

---

*Recommended for teachers: Snorri Sturluson, *The Prose Edda,* translated by Arthur Gilchrist Brodeur, N.Y.: The American-Scandinavian Foundation,

†*The Prose Edda,* p. 213.

Adverbs could be added, such as gently, softly, sorrowfully, noisily.

Children love riddles. The time before lessons, the time after lessons, and mealtimes are usually spiced with them. The children know an amazing number of riddles and they never tire of inventing more.

Children seem to relive, as did the people of the eighth and ninth centuries, the magic of a name, the power man possessed when he had the key, the knowledge of the name. A riddle uses every part of speech except the one noun, the name. There are many beautiful alliterative riddles; "The Anchor" and "The Swan" are but two of them. The children enjoy doing riddles in Eurythmy. The answers, however, must always be done silently in Eurythmy at the end of a lesson for the teacher to guess or, rather, read.

The Anchor

Old English Riddle

I war with the wind, with the waves I wrestle,
I must battle with both when the bottom I seek —
My strange habitation by surges o'er roofed.
I am strong in the strife while still I remain,
As soon as I stir they are stronger than I;
They wrench and I wrest till I run from my foes —
What was put in my keeping they carry away.
If my back be not broken I baffle them still,
The rocks are my helpers when hard I am pressed;
Grimly I grip them. Guess what I'm called?

Answer: The Anchor

The Swan

Old English Riddle

My robe is silent
When I rest on earth,
Or run by the shore, or ruffle the pools;
But oft on my pinions, upward I mount,
Borne to the skies on the buoyant air,
High over the haunts and houses of men,
Faring afar with fleeting clouds.
Then sudden my feathers are filled with music
They sing in the wind as I sail aloft,
O'er wave and wood, a wandering sprite.

Time

Riddle by a Grade 4

I am invisible,
Yet I make myself seen, heard, and felt.
I am always moving,
I never stand still.
Everyone chases me,
No one can catch me.
I am as old as the world,
Yet ever newborn.
The sun, moon, and stars direct me,
Yet my home is the earth.
What am I?

Contraction and Expansion

Contraction and expansion is a life process, a life process that should permeate every lesson. If a human being cannot breathe, he or she dies. Something dies in children if they are kept "contracted" at their desks too long. Their reaction is to fidget, wriggle, chatter, fizzle, and disrupt the lesson. Children need to stretch, move, and laugh, as well as to concentrate and be attentive.

It is possible, however, to expand while sitting at a desk. Even a dictation can give the child a breather instead of being a burden to teacher and child alike.

If the child's imagination is fired, a dictation can become a challenge, a challenge to see if a long sentence can be remembered accurately. Nine-year-olds enjoy secret messages!

Warn the children that the sentence will only be said once, and if they cannot remember it they simply leave a gap. Let the children put down their pens and listen to a short sentence, then write it; listen again, then write. The sentences can gradually become longer and longer with fewer gaps as the weeks go by.

While listening, the children expand. While writing, they concentrate. Christian Morgenstern writes in his poem about the postman:

> "My little ears are sitting on the doorstep
> Like two kittens waiting for their milk."

Listening is a healthy stretching. Children today have great difficulty in listening. We must seize every opportunity to help them learn to listen. Children so often cannot concentrate, come into themselves, because they cannot go out with their senses. They often do not sleep well because they cannot wake well. Not only Eurythmy but every lesson must be planned so that the children can experience a healthy breathing. If they are not given an opportunity to move, they cannot and will not be still.

Can Eurythmy Help English-Speaking Children to Spell?

Dr. Steiner pointed out that the spirit of the English language is in danger of being lost. This is partly because of the increasing use of phonetics. In many children's books today all the words are spelt as they are pronounced. The origin of the word, which is usually wrapped up in the spelling, is thus lost. To prevent this loss, Dr. Steiner indicated that those letters which are an essential part of the origin of the word should also be done in Eurythmy, even if they are not audible. Eurythmy teachers should bear this in mind when teaching young children. For instance, in the word "light," if the children push the clouds away with the G, watch them part and sail away with the H so that the sun can come streaming through with the T. Children will have an experience of the word that will eclipse any spelling difficulty thereafter.

It is not always possible to apply this to our English vowel sounds, but moving the letters of a word in Eurythmy does make the children aware of the many "secret" letters in our language. The children will enjoy practising so that the letters we hear are big and bold and the "secret" ones are there, but almost invisible. Thus the children's awareness is heightened, and the words imprint themselves more firmly in their memory through the imaginative quality of Eurythmy. Even musical children, who often have difficulty in retaining word pictures, can be helped in this way.

It can be utterly frustrating to a bad speller to see every third or fourth word underlined in red ink. The thought of writing every mistake out three times is deadening. Very often poor spellers write the liveliest and most beautiful compositions. I have known children who never make a spelling mistake write unimaginative essays with very little content.

Of course children must learn to spell correctly. How can we teach the poor spellers so that they do not lose heart and their writing does not lose life?

Why not write at the end of a dictation or composition: "You have made seven mistakes in the first paragraph. Try to find them. If you can't, you can ask John to help you. Write them out correctly and learn to spell them." In this way, the child's will is engaged. If they just copy corrections, they remain passive.

Words of the High One
(from The Elder Edda)

Old Norse

Young and alone on a long road,
Once I lost my way:
Rich I felt when I found another;
Man rejoices in man.

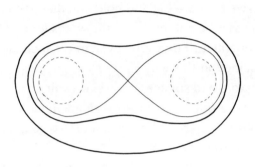

Voluspo
(from The Poetic Edda)
Translated by
Lee M. Hollander

In earliest times   did Ymir live:
Was nor sea nor land   nor salty waves,
Neither earth was there   nor upper heaven,
But a gaping nothing   and green things nowhere.

Was the land then lifted   aloft by Bur's sons
Who made Mithgard   the matchless earth;
Shone from the south   the sun on dry land,
On the ground then grew   the green sward soft.

From the south the sun, by the side of the moon,
Heaved his right hand over heaven's rim;
The sun knew not what seat he had,
The stars knew not what stead they held
The moon knew not what might she held.

Then gathered together the Gods for counsel
The holy hosts and held converse;
To night and new moon their names they gave,
The morning named, and midday also
Forenoon and evening to order the year.

Forge Me With Fire

Anonymous

Forge me with fire,
A sword for my smiting,
Fright to my foes and flames
For my fighting.

Shape me a shield,
Forceful and fierce,
Stalwart and shapely to
Fend against fears.

Strike me a spear of speed
As a shaft,
Fearless to fly as a shot
To the start.

Staunch be my front
Against fury assailed,
Strong be my soul
Where the feeble have failed.

Marwick's Song

William Morris

Barque, bravest in battle of billows and breeze,
True tower in the tempest, dry deck on the sea;
When flash the wild waters with mountains of might
You leap through the breakers with bounds of delight.

from **The Blacksmiths**

English fifteenth century

Swart, smirched smiths smattered with smoke,
Drive me to death with the din of their dents,
Such noise on nights ne'er heard men never.
Such clashing of cries and clattering of knocks.
The craftsmen clamor for coal, coal, coal!
And blow their bellows their brains to burst.

They groove and they grind and they grumble together,
Hot with heaving of heated hammers,
Of thick bull's hide are their branded aprons,
Their shanks are shod against shooting sparks.

Huge hammers they have and hard to handle,
Stark strokes strike they on the steeled stock,
Well wrought! well wrought! well wrought!
Might daunt the devil
Such life they lead,
All armourers, founders, forgemen.
Christ them save!

Steadfast I'll Stand*

Rudolf Steiner
translated from the German

Steadfast I'll stand in the world,   **Left foot.**
With certainty I'll tread the path of life,   **Right foot.**
Love, I'll cherish in the depths of my being,   **Left arm.**
Hope shall be in all my deeds,   **Right arm.**
Confidence I'll impress into my thinking.   **Head.**

Standhaft stell' ich mich ins Dasein,   **Linker Fuss.**
Sicher schreite ich die Lebensbahn,   **Rechter Fuss.**
Liebe hege ich im Wesenskern,   **Linker Arm.**
Hoffnung lege ich in all mein Tun,   **Rechter Arm.**
Vertrauen präge ich in mein Denken.   **Kopf.**

---

*Note: Given originally for the man and animal period; also suitable for Grade 5.

Unstooping

Walter de la Mare

Low on his fours the Lion
   Treads with the surly Bear;
But Men straight upward from the dust
   Walk with their heads in air;
The free sweet winds of heaven,
   The sunlight from on high
Beat on their clear bright cheeks and brows
   As they go striding by;
The doors of all their houses
   They arch so they may go,
Uplifted o'er the four-feet beasts,
   Unstooping, to and fro.

Earth Folk

Walter de la Mare

The cat she walks on padded claws,
The wolf on the hills lays stealthy paws,
Feathered birds in the rain-sweet sky
At their ease in the air, flit low, flit high.

The oak's blind, tender roots pierce deep,
His green crest towers, dimmed in sleep,
Under the stars whose thrones are set
Where never prince hath journeyed yet.

Legend

A Michael Legend from Normandy

In old days the people of "Hédé" were wont to mow their hay with scissors, and long were the hours they spent cutting the grass and piling the sheaves. The devil alone possessed a tool that could do the task in a short time. But he used it only at dead of night and flatly refused ever to lend it to anyone. The tool was certainly magic. It cut the grass in swathes, and as soon as the hay was dry it was piled into a rick.

One day Satan promised a rascally farmer of whom he had made a friend that he would mow his meadow for him the very next night. Saint Michael heard of this, and he stuck iron stakes in the ground amongst the high grass. Then he hid himself in a hollow oak and waited until the night. Only his head peeped out from the leafy branches of the tree.

About midnight he heard a whistling behind the hedge. The devil was coming. Satan stood on the fringe of the field and began to assemble his tool. He stuck it into the end of a long handle, and taking a whetstone he sharpened the edge. At last with a swinging movement he set it in motion and swiftly the grass fell in long swathes. When he struck the first iron bar, he swore like a proper devil but still continued his work. When he struck the second, his tool broke. Then he cursed, "Now my scythe is broken, I must take it to the smith." And cursing and swearing, puffing and blowing, he took it to the village of Dingé.

The next morning Saint Michael went to the smith and asked if someone had brought him a strange tool to repair. "Yes!" answered the smith, "Never before have I seen its like."

"Good! You must make me another tool exactly the same and then I will show you its use."

"Certainly," said the smith. Then he hammered away at his anvil and made a tool just like the one the devil had brought. Saint Michael showed him how to use the scythe. But he did not keep it for himself alone like the devil; he lent it to all who were in need. And soon everyone knew how to cut his grass with the scythe.

The devil was so angry that he left the country and has never been seen there since.

Plays

Harvest Masque for Grade 3*

Elmfield School

Cast of Characters

Lord of the Manor   Farmworkers

LORD OF THE MANOR: Who is standing without?
From whence do you come
With song and with shout,
With trumpet and drum?

FARMWORKERS: We come from the fields
With apples and marrows;
All the earth yields
Is heaped on our barrows.

Long have we labored
With sweat and with toil
Here is our harvest
We reaped from the soil.

LORD OF THE MANOR: O men of the fields,
Bring us your marrows,
Bring us your apples
Heaped high on the barrows.

Bring us your honey,
Your garlands of flowers,
The fruit of the earth
Of the sun and the showers.

FARMWORKERS: Gladly we come
To join in your song,
But we've ploughing to do
And we cannot stay long.

Saint Michael we honor

Note: This little masque is included as an indication of how a Grade 3 can contribute to a festival. It was a surprise to all when a teacher, about to address the whole school at Michaelmas, was rudely interrupted by loud bangings and shouting and drumming outside the assembly hall. The "secret" had been so well kept by Grade 3 that no one knew they were the men from the fields until they marched in dressed as farmers bringing the harvest festival.

Who lends us his aid,
To garner a harvest
That never will fade.

March up to "Michael Song."

• In "Autumn Saint Michael," (page 92.)

**LORD OF THE MANOR
and others:**

Dear reapers we thank you
For all that you bring
And for joy of the harvest
Pray pipe now and sing.

Iduna and the Golden Apples

Eileen Hutchins

Cast of Characters

Iduna	**Bragi**
Loki	**Asas**
Odin	**Thiassi**
Watchman	**Chorus**

SCENE 1: In Iduna's grove

CHORUS (sings):

On Asgard's height,
In the ring of the rainbow
The Asas are guarding
The fruit of gold.
Life it brings
To the weak and weary,
Love it bears
To enlight the world.

(speaks):

Odin, All-Father,
High thou art seated
Among thine Asas
In Valhall's hall.
Send thy ravens
Forth on the whirlwinds,
Bring us thy wisdom
From far and wide.

Laughter and shouting
Are far resounding
From Valhall's halls
Where the Asas feast.
But far to northward
In ice and stormwind,
The giants are keeping
Their lonely watch.

Fair are the flowers
By the sacred well,
Where the norns are weaving
Their web of fate;
But here on earth
The lands lie barren,
And who will give life
To the lonely waste?

IDUNA: My golden apples
I give in welcome,
Those who eat
Of the charmed fruit,
Lay aside
All their grief and sorrow,
Lose all their weariness
And age.

BRAGI: Lovely Iduna,
Leaving thy woodland,
Far must I fare
To the earth returning;
The flowers will be fading
The boughs will be bare,
When the music is silent,
My singing is stilled.

IDUNA: Bragi beloved,
Swift be thy speeding,
Sad is Iduna
When Bragi's away.

BRAGI: Leave not thy grove
While thy lord is away.

(Bragi departs. Thiassi and Loki enter.)

LOKI: Halt there in hiding.
Lightly I lure her
Forth from her grove
To be clasped in thy clutch.

(Thiassi hides.)

LOKI: Help me! Help me!
Heal my hurting.
My head is heavy.
My limbs are faint.
Give me to eat
Of your golden apples,
Take me to taste
Of your fairest fruit.

IDUNA: Healing and help
Stream forth from the fruit;
Take it, O Loki,
Eat and be whole.

LOKI: Wretched and wrinkled
These apples are seeming;
Far from fair
Are those by the stream.

IDUNA: Fairer than these?
That never can be.

LOKI: Come with me quickly,
I'll show you the sight.

IDUNA: I leave not the grove
While my lord is away.

LOKI: Surely one step
Is safe in my keeping.
Carry your casket,
Soon shall we see.

IDUNA: Safe in your keeping
Quickly I come.

LOKI: Behold the branches
Fair with their fruit.

(Thiassi seizes her.)

IDUNA: Help me! Help me!
Bragi beloved.
The tempest has torn me
From love and from life.

(Loki laughs.)

SCENE 2: In the grove, later

THE ASAS: Where is Iduna,
Our loveliest lady?
Lonely her grove
Where the leaves are falling.
Where has she wandered
Hence from her homeland?
The flowers are fading,
Our hearts are forlorn.

(sing): Sorrow, sorrow, sorrow for Iduna,
Lonely, lonely, stands the tree of life,
Coldly, coldly, blow the winds of winter,
Sorrow, sorrow, sorrow for our queen.

ASAS: Gray are we growing,
Wrinkled and weary,
The tree of life
Has failed of its fruit.
Bragi alone
Her best, her beloved,
He may restore her,
May rescue his queen.

(Bragi returns.)

BRAGI: Silence around me,

Earth seems to slumber.
Come, O Iduna,
To greet your lord.

Strange is the silence,
Surely she sleepeth,
Waken Iduna,
And welcome your love.

Still no answer,
Can she be hiding?
The life-tree is leafless,
Our loved one is lost.

Come forth, Loki,
Lord of all lying.
Thou hast betrayed us
With one of thy tricks.

Where hast thou lured her,
Our loveliest lady?
Tell me the truth
Or fearful thy fate.

LOKI: How should I know?
She was not in my keeping.

BRAGI: O Loki, thou liar,
Of craftiest cunning.
I see from thine eye
The deed thou hast done.

LOKI: Of her own will she wandered,
I have not hid her.

BRAGI: Then a curse shall come
To the Asas of Asgard,
All cows shall be barren,
All flocks shall fail.
Wretched and wrinkled
The gods are growing,
Shorn of their strength
Till Iduna return.

ODIN: Loki, thou liar,
Dreadful deceiver,
Speak forth thy secret,
Tell thou the truth.

LOKI: As I was hastening
Homeward to Asgard,
From the westwind a whisper
Came to my ear.

Far over the foam waves
Iduna is hidden,
Thiassi, the stormwind,
Has stolen her hence.

With my falcon's wings
I will thither be faring,
To find Iduna
And bear her back.

ODIN: With your falcon's wings
You must thither fare,
To find Iduna
And bear her back.

ASAS: Forth is he faring
On falcon's wings,
Swift is the stormwind
And bitter the blast.
Good be your going,
And lightsome, O Loki;
Strong be your striving
And swift your return.

SCENE 3: In Thiassi's stronghold

THIASSI: Come, I am kindly
Not to have killed thee.
Give me the apples,
I am thy lord.

(He seizes the casket.)

O they are shrinking,
They creep in the crannies
Get thou the apples
And give me to eat.

(She shakes her head.)

Foolish, unfaithful,
Not worthy my wooing,
It goes not to good
When Thiassi is scorned.
Forth am I faring,
To fish in the fjord,
But when I come back
You must find me the fruit,
Or else I shall clasp you,
Cramp you with coldness,
Freeze you for ever,
Firm in the ice.

(Exit.)

IDUNA: Hear me, O hear me,
Odin, All-Father,
Send forth the ravens
To harken my prayer.
Lo, from the eastward
A falcon is faring,
And hitherward, hitherward,
Hastens his flight.

(Loki appears.)

IDUNA: Loki, O false one,
Thou who betrayed me.

LOKI: Waste thou no words
But do as I say.
Wear thou these wings
Of the swift flying swallow,
Follow me hence
O'er the fields of the foam.

IDUNA: Bear me up bravely,
         O wide-spreading wings,
         Hence to my home
         To the love of my lord.

(They fly away.)

IDUNA: How far have we fared
         O'er the waves and the waters?
         Weary my wings
         And heavy my heart.

LOKI: Behind us an eagle
         Swiftly is soaring,
         Thiassi pursues us,
         Fly we more fast.

(They fly further.)

IDUNA: No more can I fly
         O'er the waves and the waters,
         Too weary my wings,
         And too heavy my heart.

LOKI: Hasten, O hasten,
         Faint not and fail not,
         Far o'er the foam waves
         Asgard I see.

SCENE 4: On Asgard's height

ASAS: Watch to the westward
         Wide o'er the waves,
         Seest thou soaring
         A falcon in flight?

WATCHMAN: Far to the westward
            Wide o'er the waves,
            The storm clouds are sweeping,
            The foam flieth far.

ASAS: Seest thou no swallow
         Or falcon in flight?

WATCHMAN: Nought but the sea mists
That sweep o'er the salt waves.

ASAS: Watch thou more warily,
Seest thou no sight?

WATCHMAN: Far o'er the foam waves
Two specks now I see,
Swift they draw nearer,
Like falcons in flight.

ASAS: Loki returneth
And with him Iduna.

WATCHMAN: Behind them an eagle
Swiftly is soaring,
One bird is now fainting
And failing in flight.

ASAS: Too far are the foam fields,
Too wide are the waves,
Their wings will now fail them,
They cannot return.

ODIN: Place thou a pile
Of logs on the hillside,
Kindle a flame
That the fire may flash.
Far o'er the foam fields
They see our great signal,
Beholding our beacon
More swiftly they strive.

LOKI: Behold now, Iduna,
Brightly there blazeth,
Fiercely there flameth
A fire from the height.
The gods are gathering
Gladly to greet us,
And bold in the midst
Is Bragi, thy lord.

ASAS: Fire! Fire!
        Leaping and soaring,
        Flaming and flashing,
        Shine afar.

This entire speech can be performed in Eurythmy.

Fire forms

        Guide our falcons
        Through the darkness,
        Waken courage,
        Make swift their flight.

**F-S-UI
almost standing**

        Fire! Fire!
        Leaping and soaring,
        Flaming and flashing
        Shine afar.

Fire forms

        Swifter, swifter,
        Swoops the eagle
        Now their strength
        Begins to fail.
        Can they reach
        The fiery beacon?
        Can they gain
        Valhalla's height?
        Bliss, bliss,
        They gain the beacon
        Now they rise
        Above the fire.

**F-S-UI
almost standing**

        Swoop to safety
        Through the smoke cloud,
        Gain their ground
        Among the gods.

        Fire! Fire!
        Burn more brightly,
        Flash more fiercely,
        Seize Thiassi,
        Clutch him closely.
        Flames enfold him,
        Fierce and full.

Fire forms

        Lo! they seize him,
        Leaping, flashing,
        Burning, blazing,

Fast enfolding,
Fiercely holding.

How he falleth,
Swiftly sweeping,   F—S—Ul   Ul
Down he crashes,
Dark and dead.

(Thiassi falls.)

ODIN: Welcome, welcome,
Fairest lady,
Lo! thy lord
Awaits thy love.
Welcome Loki,
Skilful trickster,
Once thy guile
Has served good end.
Learn, O false one,
Now for ever,
Trustier daring,
Truer speaking,
Lest thy lying
Bring us death.

CHORUS: The flame of our fire
Has laid him low,
No more will we fear
The grip of the frost.
From Thiassi's grasp
Has Iduna guarded
The golden fruit
With her heart's own warmth.
The halls of Asgard
Are far resounding
With laughter and shouting,
With light and love.

(sings):   On Asgard's height
In the ring of the rainbow,
The Asas are guarding
The fruit of gold.
Life it brings to the weak and weary,
Love it bears to enlighten the world.

Chapter Five

Grade Five (Ages Ten to Eleven)

The main lesson subjects for this year are ancient history (Indian, Persian, Babylonian, Egyptian, Greek, and Celtic), botany, biographies, geography of the homeland, arithmetic, fractions, and decimals.

There is usually an air of harmony around Grade 5. The Indian, Persian, Babylonian, Egyptian, and Greek mythologies move the children deeply and give the mood and material for the Eurythmy lessons.

When the story of the Pandava brothers is being told, a certain exercise can be introduced that relates well to the archery contest in which Arjuna alone is permitted to shoot an arrow. Dr. Steiner gave the exercise for children who have difficulty in concentrating; most children have that difficulty today.

The children stand in a line at the end of the hall. They all choose goals; at the word "go," they take aim and run swiftly toward their goal using the vowel sound I (ē) as a spear. When the teacher claps or strikes a gong, the children must stop wherever they are and stand still and upright with their I (ē) spears aiming straight ahead.

A new experience of form can be brought to the children in connection with Persian mythology and biography. This form of movement echoes something that is beginning to stir deep within the child at this time. These forms are the variations of the circle.

In the first variation, a struggle takes place between the forces within the circle and the forces outside the circle.

In the interplay, the circumference is pushed outward; the inner forces, with persevering self-assertion, battle their way into the outer world, bending and curving the line of the circle.

In the second variation, the forces outside the circle thrust their way into the circle, cutting it into jagged indentations.

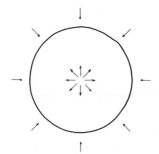  

In the first variation, the inner forces have conquered the outer ones, and in the second the outer forces have conquered the inner ones.*

In Grade 5 the Eurythmy lesson could begin with a verse, a concentration exercise, and some rod

---

*See Rudolf Steiner, *Ways to a New Style of Architecture,* Lecture 3, Anthroposophic Press, New York, 1927.

exercises. If you plan to introduce something new, it is much better to let the children sit down for this rather than stand around.

It is not a waste of time to have an occasional conversation with the children in a Eurythmy lesson. They can then understand and experience the forms better with their whole being. Perhaps you could ask the children if they can explain why so many famous people were born into poor circumstances. How is it that some people are completely crushed by outer difficulties, others are able to overcome tremendous hindrances, withstand adversities, and even gain strength in their struggles? Let the children tell you of their own experiences, or of the biographies they have read.

How can we express in movement and form the two forces that make and mold our lives? The forms could be practiced rhythmically by two groups in a circle. Every other child belongs to an inner group and faces outward, holding a rod horizontally. Each moves in curves to the next place but one. They could move in the Adonis measure. The whole circle gradually expands until the inner forces have gained mastery.   ⏤ ◡ ̔◡ ⏤

When the outer forces conquer, every other child in the circle facing inward holds a rod like a spear and lunges forward with the Paon (**uuu** ⏤), cutting into the form and causing the circle to gradually shrink.

The Persian poem of Zarathustra and the demons of darkness can be built up and practised in this way. Tennyson's "Winter" and the Eskimo Folksong are other suitable poems for this basic form.

Poems

Thus Spake Zarathustra

Persian, Seventh Century B.C.?

In the flaming fire we worship thee,
Master of Wisdom,
Lord of Light,
Ahura Mazdao,
O speak to us
In the glory of the sun,
Oh Lord of Life!

From the regions of the north,
From the regions of the north,
Forth rushed Ahriman, the deadly,
And the demons of darkness, the evildoers,
Thus spake Ahriman, the deadly deceiver.
Kill him, destroy him,
Holy Zarathustra,
Hated Zarathustra.

Thus spake Zarathustra—
The word of Ahura Mazdao is my weapon,
With his word will I strike,
The holy word of the Lord of Light
The living word of creation!

Forth fled Ahriman, the deceiver,
And the wicked, evildoing demons
Into the depths of outer darkness.

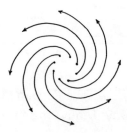

from The Bhagavad Gita

**Translated by
Edwin Arnold**

Nay but as one layeth
His worn out robes away
And taking new ones sayeth,

"These will I wear today;"
So putteth by the spirit
Lightly its garb of flesh
And passeth to inherit
A residence afresh.

Look to this Day
Sanskrit

Look to this day.
For it is life,
The very life of life:
In its brief course lie all
The realities and truths of existence,
The joy of growth,
The splendour of action,
The glory of power.
For yesterday is but a memory,
And tomorrow is only a vision.
But today well lived
Makes every yesterday a memory of happiness
And every tomorrow a vision of hope.
Look well, therefore, to this day!

Akhnaten's Hymn to Aton
Ancient Egyptian

When thou risest in the eastern horizon of heaven
Thou fillest every land with thy beauty.
When thou settest in the western horizon of heaven
The world is in darkness and as dead,

Variations of contraction and expansion.

Bright is the earth when thou risest in the horizon,
When thou shinest as Aton by day,
The darkness is banished when thou sendest forth thy rays.
How manifold are thy works,
They are hidden from before us.
O thou one God, whose powers no other possesseth.
Thou didst create the world according to thy word
While thou wast alone.
By thee men live.
When thou settest they die
The world is in thy hands
And thou art in my heart

For thou thyself art the life of time.
By thee men live
Until thou settest;
Thou makest the beauty of form,
Thou art in my heart.

Winter

Lord Alfred Tennyson

The frost is here,
The fuel is dear,
The woods are sear,
The fires burn clear,
And frost is here
And has bitten the heel of the going year.

Bite, frost, bite!
You roll away from the light
The blue woodlouse, and the plump dormouse,
And the bees are still'd, and the flies are kill'd,
And you bite far into the heart of the house,
But not into mine.

Bite, frost, bite!
The woods are all the searer,
The fuel is all the dearer,
The fires are all the clearer,
My spring is all the nearer,
You have bitten into the heart of the earth,
But not into mine.

The Christmas Rose

W. M. von Heider

What is the blossom that blooms in the snow?
The Christmas rose, the Christmas rose.

Why does it bloom when the bitter winds blow?
The Christmas rose, the Christmas rose.

It brings good tidings from paradise,
The Christmas rose, the Christmas rose.

Question and answer forms.

How can it defy the darkness and ice?
The Christmas rose, the Christmas rose.

The Christ Child's star in the center lies
Of the Christmas rose, the Christmas rose.

How can I conquer the cold and the night
Like the Christmas rose, the Christmas rose?

Fill your heart with the Christ Child's light,
Like the Christmas rose, the Christmas rose.

Song from Pippa Passes

Robert Browning

The year's at the spring,
And day's at the morn;
Morning's at seven;
The hill-side's dew-pearled:

The lark's on the wing;
The snail's on the thorn:
God's in his heaven—
All's right with the world!

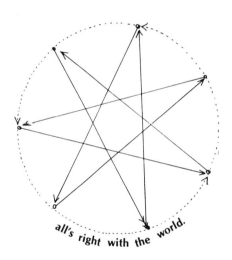

Easter Carol

Old English Carol

The world itself keeps Easter Day
And Easter larks are singing,
And Easter flowers are blooming gay,
And Easter buds are springing.
Alleluya, Alleluya!
The lord of all things lives anew
And all his works are rising too,
Hosanna in excelsis.

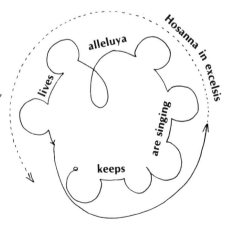

**Form based on personal
pronouns "he," "it," and
the verbs.**

Hilariter

Old English Carol

The whole bright world rejoices now,
Hilariter, hilariter,
The birds do sing on every bough,
Alleluya, alleluya.

Then shout beneath the racing skies,
Hilariter, hilariter,
To him who rose that we might rise,
Alleluya, alleluya.

And all you living things give praise,
Hilariter, hilariter,
He guideth you on all your ways,
Alleluya, alleluya.

He, Father, Son and Holy Ghost,
Hilariter, hilariter,
Our God most high, our joy and boast,
Alleluya, alleluya.

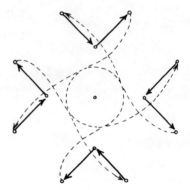

Plays

Persephone

Rosemary Gebert

Cast of Characters

Zeus	Pluto
Demeter	Persephone
Hecate	Hermes
Shades	Maidens
Mortals	Chorus

CHORUS: We tell you a story of ancient Greece
In the days when the world was young,
When on cloud-capped height of Olympus
The great gods lived in their splendor,
Immortal in beauty and wisdom.

Below on earth, eternal summer reigns,
Demeter, goddess of harvests,
Taught men to love their fruitful lands
And showed them how to till the soil
And sow and reap and working win their bread.

But far below this sunlit world of men
In caverns dark and cold where no light shone,
King Pluto ruled the underworld of shades
Alone and lonely on his rocky throne.

And now our play will show you what befell
When Pluto stole Persephone, Demeter's child,
To be his queen and share his gloomy realm.

SCENE 1: Mount Olympus, with the Underworld below

ZEUS: I am Zeus, mighty Olympian,
In wisdom I rule over gods and men.
Mine are the lightning, the winds, and the thunder,
At my command the heavens tremble and earth quakes.

PLUTO: Hail to Zeus, hurler of thunderbolts,
Hear now the voice of thy brother in Hades:
Dark is this land of the dead, and dismal,

Where whispering shadows in gloomy caverns
Sway and rustle and echo my voice.

ZEUS: Cease your complaining, dark Pluto, my brother,
Grumbling and groaning down in the depths
Marry a maiden, a daughter of men,
A bride will bring joy to the dark halls of Hades.

PLUTO: I hear your words, O Zeus, and I obey.
Shades! Prepare my journey.

FIRST SHADE: The horses are harnessed.
SECOND SHADE: The chariot waits.
THIRD SHADE: I bring your staff.
FOURTH SHADE: And I your cloak.
FIFTH SHADE: And I your cap of invisibility.
SIXTH SHADE: Made by Cyclop's skill.

PLUTO: Unseen I go, to steal a bride.

(Exit Pluto with shades. Enter Demeter and Persephone.)

SCENE 2: In the fields

DEMETER: Persephone, my mind is heavy with an unknown dread,
For me this day is dark, I know not why.

PERSEPHONE: But Mother, see, Apollo sends his brightest rays to speed the harvest.
The corn grows tall, the young fruit swells,
All mortals praise your work,
What is there to fear?

DEMETER: I do not know, and yet I fear for you.
Do not wander in the fields alone today, my daughter,
Lest harm befall you.
Stay close beside your friends till I return.

PERSEPHONE: I promise, Mother. Farewell.

DEMETER: Farewell, Persephone child; remember your promise.

(Exit Demeter. Enter maidens.)

FIRST MAIDEN: Come and dance with us, Persephone.

(Dance.)

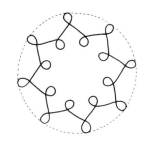

SECOND MAIDEN: Come and make garlands.

(They gather flowers and sing while making garlands.)

MAIDENS (sing):   Echo, Echo, mocking voice,
Tell me the maiden of your choice.
Naiad from her crystal pool,
Floating gracefully clear and cool?
Echo answers mockingly,
Fairest is Persephone!
Echo, Echo, mocking voice
Tell me the maiden of your choice.
Hamadryad shy and fair,
Woodland nymph with leaf-green hair?
Echo answers mockingly,
Fairest is Persephone.

(Dance.)

(Persephone wanders picking flowers. Enter Pluto unseen, conjures up magic flowers.)

PERSEPHONE: From flower to flower I wander on
And there is one more fair than all the rest—
Strange, I cannot pick it.

(Pluto grasps her hand.)

Mother! Mother!

(Pluto strikes the earth—thunder sounds.)

PLUTO: Open ye rocks!
Thus plunging deep we ride
Down to the Underworld I bear my bride.

MAIDENS: Persephone, she's gone,
Demeter, O Demeter.

SCENE 3: In the fields, later

(Music. Enter Demeter carrying a torch.)

DEMETER: Sad is my heart, hopeless is my quest,
The whole wide world I've searched in vain
Come back, come back, Persephone,
I call, but no one answers me.

(Enter mortals. Kneel before Demeter.)

MORTALS: Mother of harvests, hear our cry:
Our fields are barren,
Our cattle pine,
Our grapes are withered,
Our children starve.
Mother of harvests, still your grief
And help us—or we die.

DEMETER: Poor mortals, all your needs I know,
But Pluto stole Persephone, stole all my power too.
My heart is cold,
My hands are numb,
And if Persephone is dead
The earth dies with her.

(Enter Hecate.)

HECATE: Persephone yet lives;
Through my gloomy gates she passed,
Prisoner of Pluto's power,
Sharing dark Hades throne.
She weeps and mourns the sunlit world she loves.

MORTALS: Through Hecate's dark gates may none return,
And we are doomed to die;
Great Zeus, have pity on us now
For you alone can save us.

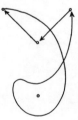

(Mortals and Hecate dance to sad music.)

SCENE 4: Mount Olympus, with the Underworld below

ZEUS: The prayers of mortals sigh about our ears,
               We must save Persephone.
               Hermes, swift messenger, go quickly now
               And bring Demeter's daughter
               Back from the Underworld.

HERMES: O mighty Zeus, I go!
               Let your lightnings speed my winged feet.
               Courage, Demeter.
               Zeus has commanded me
               To bring your daughter back to you.

               (Exit. Shades enter Underworld, leading Persephone to throne.)

PLUTO: Do not weep, sweet queen.
               Come shades, dance to cheer my bride
               Night and day she weeps and pines
               And neither eats nor drinks,
               My poor pale bride;
               Taste this pomegranate
               Sunripe and sweet.

               (Enter Hermes as she bites.)

HERMES: Eat it not, Persephone!
               By the command of mighty Zeus
               I come to take you home.
               Be gone, you shivering shades,
               And whisper comfort to your lord
               Who shrinks and cowers from the light of day,
               Come!

               (Hermes leads her away.)

SCENE 5: In the fields

DEMETER: Persephone!

PERSEPHONE: Mother, I never thought to see you more!

DEMETER: Brother Zeus, my thanks—

And thanks to Hermes, trusty messenger.
Beloved child, welcome home,
I trust you did not eat of Pluto's fare?

PERSEPHONE: I ate only four seeds of a pomegranate.

ZEUS: Four seeds too many! Now hear my decree:
Of each twelve months Persephone must pass

(Enter Pluto.)

Four in the Underworld as Pluto's bride,
To pay with sorrow for the seeds she took;
The other eight are hers to spend
On earth in sunlight and in happiness.

(Persephone stands hand in hand with Demeter and Pluto.)

CHORUS: Now all is well, as wise Zeus has decreed.
For when Persephone is in the Underworld
It's winter on the earth;
The flowers die down,
The trees are bare,
All nature sleeps.
And when Persephone returns
The spring comes with her.
Flowers bloom,
The crops begin to grow
In sun and rain.

And so the seasons come and go
And men give thanks to the immortal gods,
Who set their lives
Within the changing year.

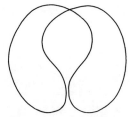

Chapter Six

Grade Six (Ages Eleven to Twelve)

Subjects for this year are Greco-Roman history to the beginning of the fifteenth century, physics (light, heat, sound), geometry, geography (regions of the world and geology), gymnastics and athletics, woodwork, and gardening.

This is the time when every teacher surely breathes a word of thanks to the Spartans. Aches and pains are there "to be endured" without flinching; certain dislikes and "allergies" such as spinach and rice pudding can now be bravely overcome; unpopular lessons are a challenge; dictations are tests of memory, especially if the teacher states firmly that he or she will only say each sentence once. It is even possible to remain quiet for long periods. Spartans are strong and silent. Spartans never moan.

The children demand to be tested at this age. They hate Eurythmy if they are allowed to do it badly. They like to be called upon to do exercises alone, or in small groups in front of the rest of the class to show how precisely they can do it. They like to have a star by their name in the Eurythmist's register if they have done well. They will enjoy doing concentration exercises in this way. As a grand challenge, occasionally half the class can do a concentration exercise (1234, 1234, 1234, 1234, 1234, and so on) while the rest of the class sits in a wide ring around and, at a given sign, shouts and tries to put them off by counting wrongly. This is indeed a concentration test that puts them on their metal.

If the Greek athlete fires the children's imagination at this time and becomes their hero, he can in some measure prevent the boys and girls whose legs and arms are growing at an alarming rate from lolling and becoming weighed down by their bodies.

As the children enter into adolescence, there is often a tendency toward circulation disorders. This can be alleviated and indeed prevented by working strongly with rhythms—classical Greek rhythms. In conjunction, as always, with the lessons of the class teacher, Greek rhythms can be practiced and performed as a play without words, accompanied by cymbals, drums, triangles, and the like.

The gods descend from Olympus to mingle with men, stepping to the rhythm of the dactyl. The priests bear palm leaves as a sun symbol, pomegranates as an earth symbol (expansion and contraction) in solemn procession, walking in spondees. The warriors go to battle with energetic anapests, the women mourn those slain in battle with tragic anapests, and so on. Different forms can be introduced for the different rhythms. The children can take it in turns, playing the percussion instruments most suited to the rhythms.

Geometrical forms and rod exercises should be practiced. This is the time when the pupils can begin to experience the life forces as bearers of thought. The children can be told, for instance, to do the rod exercise down, up, right, and left, without moving their arms; to send their thoughts and feelings deep down below the plant cover of the earth and then up to the heights of the sky, to the right and to the left, and so on. Then let the rod follow the inner movement. The children will find that if they anticipate the movement in this way, by sending their thoughts ahead like pioneers or bridge builders, their arms will not ache—however long the exercise lasts! They are quite capable of doing "inner gymnastics" with their thoughts at this age.

Anticipation means to enjoy in advance. Whatever we do with joy, we do with our whole being. In moving with anticipation we begin to learn a skill. We begin to experience the movement of the life forces that precedes our every physical movement. Children can sometimes "understand" the three elements of Eurythmy (movement-thought, feeling, and character-will) better than adults.

It is good to work hard on the Dance of Peace and the Dance of Energy during the story of the Trojan Wars. In a play, for instance, the Greeks could perform the Dance of Energy before entering into the great horse. The Trojans, believing the war to be over and won, could perform the Dance of Peace.

These two Dionysian "dances" must always have a center from which strength and courage or all-pervading peace can flow. In the Peace Dance, the sounds should rise up like smoke from the altar fire. These educational dances strengthen the children's ability to work and to work together.

Just as little children need the interval of the fifth, and the nine-year-olds the major and minor third, so now when the children are coming deeper into their physical organization, they need the octave to uplift them. Rudolf Steiner calls the experience of the octave, "the finding of one's self at a higher level."

After the children have learned and lived in the experience of the octave, the other intervals can be taught in connection with the main lesson on acoustics. The intervals are an inner musical experience. Imaginative pictures are quite unnecessary and can hinder the listening that must now be set in motion.

Greek Rhythms

Dactyl — UU (finger): This is the rhythm of the gods descending to the world of men to teach and to ordain.

Iambic U —: The spear thrust
Trochee — U: The step of Mercury
Amphibrachus U—U: The rhythm of the nymphs and dryads and the attendants of the goddess of spring (strewing flowers); a joyous rhythm.

Spondeus A Majore ´— — and A Minore — —´: A solemn rhythm, the rhythm of the priests bearing wine to pour before the gods; of the patricians in procession to make a treaty or an alliance; priests carrying palms as a sun symbol, pomegranates as an earth symbol.

Proceleusmaticus ´UUUU (together ´UUUU): To rouse, to urge.

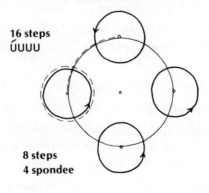

16 steps
ÚUUU

8 steps
4 spondee

Anapest **UU —** : The step that carries us upward, onward; the rhythm that leads us back to the gods; the rhythm of sorrow and joy, struggle and peace.

Hexameter **—UU—UU—UU ⌒ —UU—UU—UU ⌒** : Harmony; the rhythm of the great epics.

Poems

In May
Anonymous

In May I go a-walking to hear the linnet sing,
The blackbird and the throstle, a-praising God the King;
It cheers the heart to hear them, to see the leaves unfold
And the meadows scattered over with buttercups of gold.

Rhythms

The Fugitives
Percy Bysshe Shelley

The waters are flashing,
The white hail is dashing,
The lightnings are glancing,
The hoarspray is dancing—
    Away!

Amphibrachus: good for sanguine children (U — U).

U—

The whirlwind is rolling,
The thunder is tolling,
The forest is swinging,
The minster bells ringing
    Come away!

UU—

The earth is like ocean,
Wreck-strewn and in motion:
Bird, beast, man and worm
Have crept out of the storm
    Come away!

Fairy Song
from **Midsummer Night's Dream**
William Shakespeare

Over hill, over dale,
Thorough bush, thorough briar,
Over park, over pale,
Thorough flood, thorough fire,
I do wander everywhere,
Swifter than the moon's sphere;
And I serve the Fairy Queen,
To dew her orbs upon the green.
The cowslips tall her pensioners be;
In their gold coats spots you see;
Those be rubies, fairy favors,
In those freckles live their savors:
I must go seek some dewdrops here,
And hang a pearl in every cowslip's ear.

**Anapest followed by
changing rhythm**

from **A Song About Myself**
John Keats

There was a naughty boy
And a naughty boy was he,
He ran away to Scotland
The people for to see—
Then he found
That the ground
Was as hard,
That a yard
Was as long,
That a song
Was as merry,
That a cherry
Was as red—
That lead
Was as weighty,
That fourscore
Was as eighty,
That a door
Was as wooden
As in England—
So he stood in his shoes
And he wonder'd,
He wonder'd,

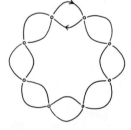

He stood in his shoes
And he wonder'd.

Hie Away!
Sir Walter Scott

Hie away, hie away!
Over bank and over brae,
Where the copsewood is the greenest,
Where the fountains glisten sheenest,
Where the lady fern grows strongest,
Where the morning dew lies longest,
Where the blackcock sweetest sips it,
Where the fairy latest trips it:
Hie to haunts right seldom seen,
Lovely, lonesome, cool, and green:
Over bank and over brae,
Hie away, hie away!

War Song of the Saracens
James Elroy Flecker

We are they who come faster than fate,   **Anapest**
We are they who ride early or late.
We storm at your ivory gate
Pale Kings of the Sunset, beware!
Not in silk nor in samet we lie,
Not in curtained solemnity die
Among women who chatter and cry,
And children who mumble a prayer.
But we sleep by the ropes of the camp,
And we rise with a shout, and we tramp
With the sun or the moon for a lamp,
And the spray of the wind in our hair.

Pandora's Song
from "The Fire-bringer"
William Vaughn Moody

Of wounds and sore defeat
I made my battle stay;   **Iambic**
Winged sandals for my feet
I wove of my delay;
Of weariness and fear

I made my shouting spear;
Of loss and doubt and dread,
And swift oncoming doom
I made a helmet for my head
And a floating plume.

from **Pandora**

Johann Wolfgang von Goethe

Kindle the fire flames,
Fire the first of names,
Highest achieved he
Who robbed the spark.
He who has kindled it
And subjugated it,
Forges it, molds it to
Crowns for the head.

Hercules

Eileen Hutchins

Who is this who cometh as in conquest?
Strong he strides and free.
Light of glory gleams around his temples,
More than man is he.

Dark has been the danger of his daring,
Fierce the fight and fell;
None can know the fashion of his faring
Hither out of hell.

Who is this who cometh as in conquest?
Strong he strides and free.
Light of glory gleams around his temples,
Man and god is he.

from **Hymn to the Earth**

Verse 4
Samuel Taylor Coleridge

Earth! Thou mother of numberless children, the nurse and the mother,   **Hexameter**
Sister, thou of the stars, and beloved by the Sun, the rejoicer!
Guardian and friend of the Moon, O Earth, whom the comets forget not,
Yea, in the measureless distance wheel round and again they behold thee!

from **Andromeda**

Charles Kingsley

Over the mountain aloft ran a rush and a roll and a roaring;   Hexameter
Downward the breeze came indignant, and leapt with a howl to the water,
Roaring in cranny and crag, till the pillars and clefts of the basalt
Rang like a god-swept lyre, and her brain grew mad with the noises;
Crashing and lapping of waters, and sighing and tossing of weed beds,
Gurgle and whisper and hiss of the foam, while thundering surges
Boomed in the wave-worn halls, as they champed at the roots of the mountain.

The Craft of a Keeper of Sheep

**Moschus, translated from
the Greek by Ernest Myers**

Would that my father had taught me the craft of a keeper of sheep,   Hexameter
For so in the shade of the elm tree, or under the rocks on the steep
Piping on reeds I had sat, and had lulled my sorrow to sleep.

Written in March

William Wordsworth

The cock is crowing,
The stream is flowing,
The small birds twitter,
The lake doth glitter,
The green field sleeps in the sun;

The oldest and youngest
Are at work with the strongest;
The cattle are grazing,
Their heads never raising;
There are forty feeding like one!

Like an army defeated
The snow hath retreated,
And now doth fare ill
On the top of the bare hill;
the ploughboy is whooping—anon—anon.

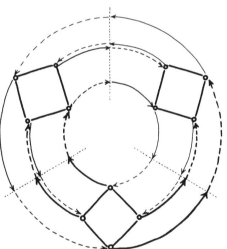

Transitions of Square

There's joy in the mountains;
There's life in the fountains;
Small clouds are sailing,
Blue sky prevailing,
The rain is over and gone!

from **Chanticleer**

William Austin

All this night shrill chanticleer,
Day's proclaiming trumpeter,
Claps his wings and loudly cries,
Mortals, mortals, wake and rise!

See a wonder
Heav'n is under;
From the earth is risen a Sun
Shines all night, though day be done.

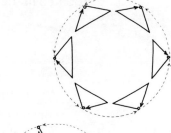

Wake, O earth, wake ev'rything!
Wake and hear the joy I bring;
Wake and joy; for all this night
Heav'n and ev'ry twinkling light,

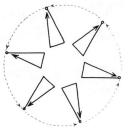

All amazing,
Still stand gazing.
Angels, Powers, and all that be,
Wake, and joy this Sun to see.

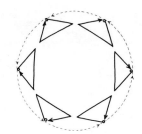

Laudes Creaturarum Quas Fecit Beatus Franciscus

from "**Hymn to the Sun**"

Saint Francis

WIND: Laudato sii, mi signore,
Per frate vento
Et per aere et nubilo
Et sereno et omne tempo
Per lo quale a le tue creature
Dai sustentamento.

WATER: Laudato sii, mi signore,
Per sora aqua,

La quale ĕ multo utile et humile
Et pretiosa et casta.

FIRE: Laudato sii, mi signore,
Per frate focu,
Per lo quale ennallumini la nocte,
Et ello ĕ bello et jocundo
Et robustoso et forte.

EARTH: Laudato sii, mi signore,
Per sora nostra matre terra
La quale ne sustenta e governa
Et produce diversi fructi
Con colorti flori et herba.

The Ride-by-Nights

Walter de la Mare

Up on their brooms the witches stream,
Crooked and black in the crescent's gleam;
One foot high, and one foot low,
Bearded, cloaked, and cowled, they go.
'Neath Charlie's Wain they twitter and tweet,
And away they swarm 'neath the Dragon's feet.
With a whoop and a flutter they swing and sway,
And surge pell-mell down the Milky Way.
Betwixt the legs of the glittering Chair,
They hover and squeak in the empty air.
Then round they swoop past the glimmering Lion
To where Sirius barks behind huge Orion;
Up, then, and over to wheel amain,
Under the silver, and home again.

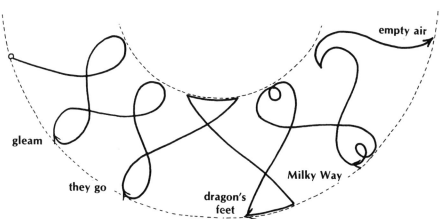

All Hallow's Eve
Edinburgh School

All Hallow's Eve it is tonight;
Out come witches, elves, and sprite.
Beware, beware of spook and spell,
They'll get you if you don't watch well.

Plays

The Lord of Lorn
Eileen Hutchins

Cast of Characters

Herald	King of France
Lady of Lorn	Queen of France
Lord of Lorn	Their daughter, the princess
Their only child	Nurse
(later, Disaware)	Servant to the princess
Steward	Head groom
Shepherd	Scottish and French knights
His wife	Chorus
Porter at the King of France's Court	

CHORUS: From Scotland a noble youth rode forth,
To France did he wend his way,
Yet wronged was he without remorse
And forced as shepherd boy to stay.
But the truth, like the sun, will arise-o,
But the truth, like the sun, will arise.

SCENE 1: At the court of the Earl of Lorn

HERALD: (*Fanfare*) At the court of the Scottish Earl of Lorn.

CHORUS: It was the worthy Lord of Lorn,
He was a lord of high degree,
And he would send his only son
Abroad to learn civility.

LADY OF LORN: Who shall go with him on his way?
For husband, we have none but he.

LORD: Madam, my steward shall go with him,
For he is true to you and me.

LADY: Come hither, steward, and take this purse
Of gold for you and for our son;
And I will give you twice as much,
When that your task is truly done.

STEWARD: If I be false to my young lord
Then God be so to me indeed.
I vow to take him safe to France
And bring him to the King with speed.

SCENE 2: In France

CHORUS: They journey over field and fell;
They ride across the barren moor;
They traverse wild and stormy seas
Until of France they reach the shore.

CHORUS: And then upon their lonely road
The steward draws his deadly knife,
His wicked plan he now unfolds
To rob the lad and take his life.

BOY: O mercy, steward, by God's good grace,
By Mary Queen, have pity on me,
I pray thee, grant to me my life,
And all I have I'll give to thee.

STEWARD: Then take thou off that crimson cloak,
That satin doublet rich and rare,
And do thou doff that velvet hat,
And give to me thy shoes so fair.

And thou'lt swear upon thy knee
By God that reigns in heaven so high,
To no man shalt thou tell the tale
Of who thou art, or thou shalt die.

BOY: I swear to thee upon my knee
                     By God that reigns in heaven so high,
                     To no man will I tell the tale
                     Of who I am, for fear I die.

STEWARD: And now put on this kelten coat
                     And these drab hose so rough to see;
                     And thou shalt go to yon shepherd's house
                     And tend his sheep upon the lea.

BOY: And what henceforth shall be my name?
                     Prithee, good steward, tell to me.

STEWARD: Thy name shall be poor Disaware,
                     Who tends the sheep on a lonely lea.

SCENE 3: At the shepherd's house

BOY: Good shepherd, do you need a lad
                     To tend your sheep on the lonely lea?

SHEPHERD: Now who art thou who comes so late,
                     And asks to tend my sheep for me?

BOY: O, I am only poor Disaware,
                     A shepherd lad of poor degree.

SHEPHERD: We have no child to give us aid,
                     So welcome here most readily.

WIFE: Thou shalt be our son and dwell with us,
                     A mother's care I'll give to thee.

CHORUS: He stays with them in the shepherd's hut
                     And tends their sheep on the lonely lea.
                     But ever again he makes his moan
                     That his father and mother he'll never see.

                     The wicked steward goes on his way,
                     At last he comes to the court of France;
                     He calls himself the heir of Lorn,
                     To make a fortune he takes his chance.

SCENE 4: The French court

HERALD:	(*Fanfare*) At the court of the King of France.
STEWARD:	O porter, go and tell your king The heir of Lorn now seeks his grace.
PORTER:	Your Majesty, the heir of Lorn Within your court now seeks a place.
KING:	I welcome thee, O heir of Lorn, I hold your father in high esteem. Pray greet this stranger, my daughter dear, Now give him welcome, my noble queen.

(The queen greets him, the daughter bears a drink to him, and they talk aside.)

KING (to Queen):	We need alliance with Scotland's throne, And the Lord of Lorn is of high degree. It would be fitting to wed our daughter To this young earl from across the sea. O come to me, thou son of Lorn; If thou wilt wed my daughter dear, Thou shalt be heir of half my land And have three thousand pounds a year.
STEWARD:	O gladly will I wed your daughter, And all you ask me will I do.
KING:	Before me, now you plight your troth And vow to be for ever true, Until the wedding bells shall ring And priests shall bless this union now.

(The betrothed couple withdraw.)

NURSE:	I do not like this hurried match I cannot trust this stranger's tongue, For yesternight I had a dream — A carrion crow flew o'er the sun.

QUEEN: O nurse, you grow too old and sour,
We cannot listen to foolish dreams.

KING: You cannot judge affairs of state;
You know not what this marriage means.

(Princess and steward come forward.)

PRINCESS: O, I would see the roebuck run
Through hill and dale and forest free.

STEWARD: My dearest lady, be it so,
A-hunting thou shalt go with me.

SCENE 5: Near the shepherd's house

(They ride round; Disaware comes, sits at the side.)

DISAWARE **(sings):** My father is the Lord of Lorn,
While I sit here in poverty—
My mother and he are far away
And know not what has become of me.
May the truth, like the sun, soon arise-o
May the truth, like the sun soon arise.

(Plays the pipe.)

PRINCESS: Go, fetch me hither yon shepherd boy,
I want to know what he doth say.

SERVANT: My lady calls you to speak with her,
Her bidding you must now obey.

(Disaware kneels to her.)

PRINCESS: What is thy name? Where wast thou born?
For whose sake makest thou this moan?

DISAWARE: I am Disaware, in Scotland born,
And I mourn one dead these years agone.

PRINCESS: Tell me of Scotland, thou handsome lad,
And now the truth I ask of thee,

Knowest thou there the young Lord of Lorn
Who has come to France a-wooing me?

DISAWARE: Yes, that I do indeed, fair madam,
I know that lord, yea, verily,
The Lord of Lorn is a worthy earl,
If he were at home in his own country.

PRINCESS: Wilt thou leave thy sheep, thou bonny lad,
And come in service unto me?

DISAWARE: I thank you madam, I will indeed,
And at your bidding I will be.

SCENE 6: The royal stables

CHORUS: The King of France approves the lad,
The youth is handsome for to see.
Since Disaware loves horses well,
Groom of the stable he comes to be.

HEAD GROOM: O here comes a lady's lad—
Look at his hands, so white and fair!
He needs to sleep amidst the mire
And feel the straws amongst his hair.

(He throws sticks and straws over the lad and trips him up. Disaware brings water for the horse.)

DISAWARE: Now come, thou gelding, take thy drink,
I brought it from the well so free.

(The gelding tosses its head and strikes him.)

DISAWARE: Woe worth thee, gelding, for thy deed,
And woe to the mare that foaled thee.
Thou little knowest, the Lord of Lorn
Thou hast stricken, a lord of high degree.

PRINCESS: Sing on thy song, thou stable groom,
I will release thee of thy pain.

DISAWARE: Nay, Lady, I have made an oath,
               I dare not tell my tale again.

PRINCESS: Sing on thy song then to thy gelding,
               And so thy oath shall saved be.

DISAWARE   (to the horse): I am the heir of the Lord of Lorn;
               The wicked steward has ousted me.

PRINCESS   (going to the King):
               Put off my wedding, O Father dear,
               Put off my wedding these months three,
               For I am sick and like to die;
               And let my nurse now care for me.

CHORUS: The Lady she has written a letter
               Full speedily with her own hand.
               She has sent it to the Lord of Lorn
               To where he dwells in fair Scotland.

SCENE 7: At the Scottish court

HERALD: (*Fanfare*) At the Court of the Scottish Earl of Lorn.

LADY: O woe is me, for our only son.
               O woe is me, for that wicked wight.

               (She weeps and wrings her hands.)

LORD: Now stop your tears, my Lady of Lorn,
               We'll be avenged with all our might.

CHORUS: The Lord calls up his merry men,
               They ride and sail to France full fast.
               And there they seek the king's own court
               And there the trumpet sounds its blast.

SCENE 8: At the French court

               (Fanfare. The Scottish knights meet Disaware at the stable. They kneel to him; he joins his father.)

LORD: The Lord of Lorn here claims his rights

And for dire vengeance doth he call.
Hand over that traitor without delay
And he shall be hanged before you all.

CHORUS: O seize the traitor and bind him fast,
O capture him, thou stable groom.

SINGLE VOICE: Lo, there he stands on the castle wall—
And now he leaps to his certain doom!

KING: All thanks to thee, thou Lord of Lorn
That thou has freed us from villainy.

LORD: We'll have a marriage before we go,
If thou art half as willing as we.

KING: O heir of Lorn, if thou'lt marry my daughter,
Ten thousand crowns I'll give to thee.

BOY: I'd rather have her with a ring of gold
Than all the treasure you offer me.

FINAL CHORUS: Thus ends the story of the Lord of Lorn,
Who bravely faced death upon his way
And thus won leadership and grace
And wed a maiden, bright as day.
For the truth, like the sun, will arise-o,
For the truth, like the sun, will arise.

Chapter Seven

Grades Seven and Eight
(Ages Twelve to Fourteen)

The main lesson subjects for Grade 7 are the history of Europe from the fifteenth to the seventeenth centuries, the study of the stars, nutrition and hygiene, physics (acoustics, optics, heat, magnetism, mechanics, and electricity), and equations.

In Grade 8, the main lesson subjects are history up to modern times, physiology, physics (hydraulics, aeromechanics, climatology, and meterorology), chemistry, and solid geometry. (Geometry and mathematics are continued.)

After the child's twelfth year, a great change takes place, comparable to the change after the ninth year. During this change, however, children seem to become imprisoned in their bodies, bodies that are becoming heavy and discordant.

The boys grow clumsy and awkward. Many of them begin to dislike the inner activity of movement demanded in Eurythmy, especially if they are ardent television viewers. They prefer to keep their hands in their pockets. The girls are usually physically more pliant, but they tend to chatter and giggle. The increasing ability of the children to use their intellect, to think logically, and to understand cause and effect manifests itself in individual ways. They begin to question much that was previously taken for granted. They become acutely conscious of how the teacher tackles difficult situations. There is a new understanding between teacher and child, and new recognition of each other is demanded.

In recent years, a very genuine fear has begun to seep down below the surface of the child's everyday life—a fear and a sense of helplessness and hopelessness.

The young person of today is very much aware of modern problems such as pollution, famine, synthetic versus organic food production, political unrest, unemployment, medical and sociological questions and experiments, and the like. Radio, television, films, and newspapers, and sometimes even the parents' interest or lack of interest can give children the fearful feeling, "There is nothing I can do about it, I might as well give up!" This is the feeling of futility in many young people today. There is an awakening to the world around them and a deep need for gathering protection.

Just as at the age of nine the curriculum could give children the sense of security they needed, so now at the age of twelve to fourteen (those difficult years when the soul-spirit is beginning to free itself from the physical body and body of formative life forces) the curriculum can help children gain courage of heart and clarity of thought. Apart from the main lesson subjects in the sciences (acoustics, optics, heat, magnetism, electricity, and the fundamental laws of mechanics and chemistry), the discovery and rise of natural science in the seventeenth century make a deep impression, bringing the realization of cause and effect in our own times. The main lessons on hygiene, nutrition, and health also bring the answers to many of the questions rumbling within the young people at this time.

The gymnastics started in Grade 6, with exercises, give the children a healthy control of their bodies.

Gardening, which in many schools has been neglected and considered impractical, will have to take pride of place in the future, for this is one of the subjects in which children can experience that there is something they can do.

Young people who have so much physical strength and no means of using it become destructive, self-centered, and indolent, and they cease to care. Eurythmy, gymnastics, and games are not adequate. Children no longer walk to school; they are driven to the doorstep, they **sit** at their lessons, they are driven home, and they **sit** down again, either to watch television or to do homework. They have tremendous strength and energy that are not being used. Their thinking processes tend to stagnate if they are not required to use their limbs. Planting trees, felling trees, leveling ground, ditching and digging, even sandpapering and polishing desks, give the children of this age a sense of achievement and well-being.

Work on a farm or in forestry for short periods is being introduced in some schools. This is proving beneficial to the physical and mental development of the child.

What has this to do with the teaching of Eurythmy? What is the task of the Eurythmist in Grades 7 and 8?

If it is at all possible and schedules permit, both Eurythmists and children win confidence in each other if the Eurythmist takes a real interest not only in the main lesson subjects but especially in the gymnastics, games, gardening, and woodwork lessons. Watch and cheer the children running, jumping, and vaulting. Go into the garden, and let them explain the work they are doing. This can be done after school hours! Go and admire newly polished desks or their woodwork. Get to know the children as individuals and realize their individual needs. This is difficult in a large school, but not impossible. The Eurythmist's attitude at this time can make or mar the Eurythmy lessons. This is a time when Eurythmy could give them the answers to many of their problems.

After Grade 6, a class often tends to separate into small groups. The boys get together; the girls get together. They divide up into even smaller groups as cliques are formed, and there are invariably some who are "out of it" and do not belong to any group.

As boys and girls grow older, their individual abilities in languages, mathematics, gymnastics, and so on become more varied. Some boys and girls cannot keep up, others want to go ahead. Some like Eurythmy, others feel awkward and dislike it. The teachers too, in some schools, find it necessary to divide the class into upper and lower math groups, upper and lower language groups. There are extra lessons in English for some, which others do not need. The class seems about to disintegrate. Then, as often as not, "the play's the thing,"—a play in which several teachers work together, in which there are acting parts and Eurythmy parts, and in which stagecraft can be taught (when to move forward or backward, how to do stage makeup, and so on). Some pupils can make scenery and costumes, others can be the music makers or do the lighting. The whole class can become involved in creating a work that can be presented to the school.

In Grade 7, the Tone Eurythmy is of great importance, especially work with the intervals, which will have begun in Grade 6 in connection with the main lesson on "sound." Now is the time also to introduce the beat and bar line. The young people can experience the mechanics of their own bony systems; they can, as it were, grasp their own skeletons as they beat time with their arms and alternate between the right and left in their steps. Beat, rhythm, and melody can be practised in three groups.

When practising the rotations and inversions of triangles, squares, pentagons, and so on, each pupil moves at a different tempo and has an individual path, and yet together they create a harmonious construction. They can also practise rod exercises with geometrical forms, as well as the movements for sympathy, antipathy, yes and no, and the head and foot positions.

Poems

The Name of Man
Russian Legend

In eight parts God made Man;
From the earth He took his bones,
From the sea, his blood,
From the sun, beauty,
From the clouds, thoughts,
From the wind, his breath,
From the stones, strength and grace,
From the light, humility,
From the Spirit, wisdom.

And when God had created Man
There was as yet no name for him.
The heights of Heaven are the Father
The circle of Earth is the Son.
The depths of the sea, the Holy Spirit.
But God's creation, Man, had as yet no name.

And God called the four archangels,
Michael, Gabriel, Uriel, Raphael,
And God said to the archangels;
Go forth and seek the name of Man.

Michael went to the east
And came to the star Anathos,
He took from him the Ah
And brought it unto God.

Gabriel wandered to the west
And saw the star Disis,
He took from him the D
And brought it unto God.

Uriel turned toward midnight
And met the star Aratus [Arktus],
He took from him the Ah
And brought it unto God.

Raphael sped toward midday
And beheld the star Mebrie [Mesebria],

He took from him the M
And brought it unto God.

And God commanded Michael
To speak the Word, the name of Man,
And Michael spake A D A M,
And Adam was the first Man on Earth.

Eurythmy: Diagrams by Elke Worm-Jacobs

Grade 3 stand in one circle for:

"In eight parts God made Man"

Move into two circles by the pause.   **Circle contracts.**

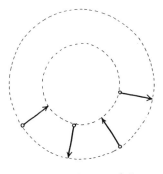

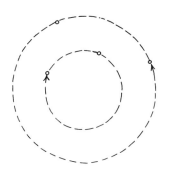

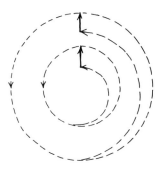

"From the earth"   "From the sea"   "From the sun"

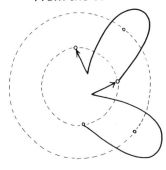

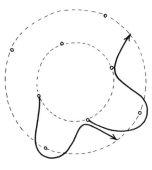

"From the clouds"   "From the wind"   "From the stones"   **(standing)**

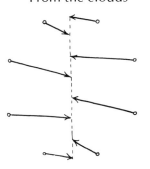

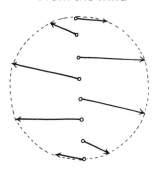

"From the light"   "From the Spirit"

(Exit Grade 3.)

Grade 7 enter and stand in a circle for:

"And when God had created Man
There was yet no name for him"

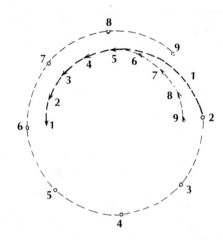

"The heights of Heaven are the Father"

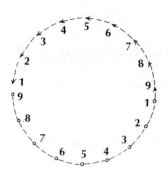

"The circle of Earth is the Son"

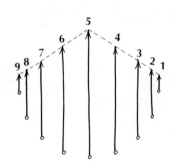

"The depths of the sea, the Holy Spirit"

Enter Archangels in the pause.

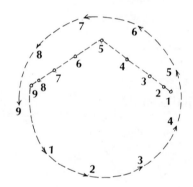

"But God's creation, Man, had as yet no name"

(standing)

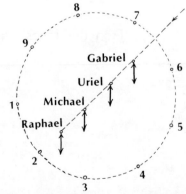

"And God called the four archangels,
Michael, Gabriel, Uriel, Raphael"

Circle takes 1 step forward on "called"

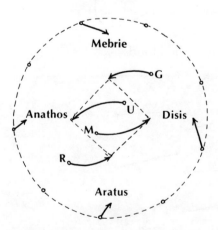

"And God said to the archangels:
Go forth and seek the name of Man"

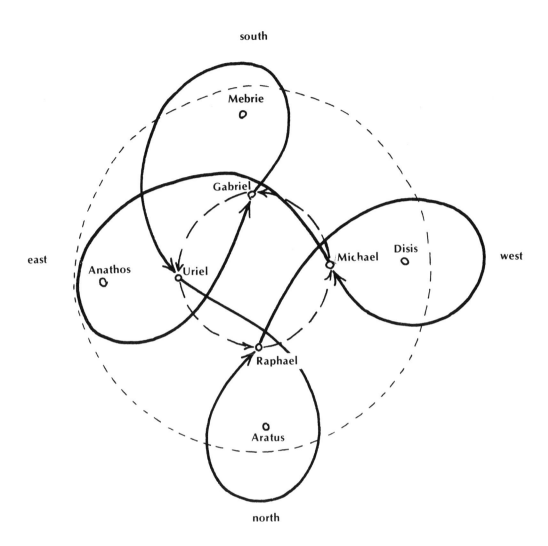

south

Mebrie
o

Gabriel

Disis
Michael o

east   west

Anathos
o

Uriel

Raphael

o
Aratus

north

"Michael . . . God."	**Alone.**
	All silently, two places around the inner circle.
"Gabriel . . . God."	**Repeat form for each Archangel.**
"Uriel . . . God."	
"Raphael . . . God."	
	All together the lemniscate.
	Michael comes forward and does the word. "Adam." **Alone.**
"And Adam . . . Earth."	**The sounds together standing.**

Eskimo Folksong

The great sea has set me in motion,
Set me adrift,
And I move as the weed in the river.
The arch of the sky
And the mightiness of storms
Encompasses me;

And I am left,
Trembling with joy.

Magic Song for Him Who Wishes to Live
Thule Eskimo

Day arises
From its sleep,
Day wakes up
With the dawning light.
Also you must arise,
Also you must awake
Together with the day
Which comes.

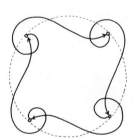

The Lights

American Indian (Lada)

The sun is a luminous shield
Born up the blue path
    By a god.

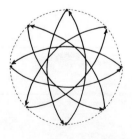

The moon is the torch
Of an old man
    Who stumbles over stars.

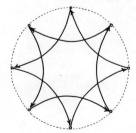

We Are the Stars
American Indian

We are the stars that sing,
We sing with our light,
We are the birds of fire,
We fly across the heavens:
Our light is a star.

from Thunder Drums
Chippewa War Dance

Beat on the buckskins, beat on the drums,
Hi, Hi, Hi! for the Thunderbird comes;
His eyes burn red with the blood of battle,
His wild wings roar in the medicine rattle.
Thunderbird-god, while our spirits dance
Tip with your lightning the warrior's lance.

Beat, beat on the drums,
For the Thunderbird comes.

Hay-yah-ah-hay!
Hay-yah-ah-hay!

Hymn to the Pole Star
Anonymous

Constellations come and climb the heaven and go
And thou dost see them rise,
Star of the pole! and thou do'st see them set,
Alone in thy cold skies,
Thou keepest thine old unmoving station yet.

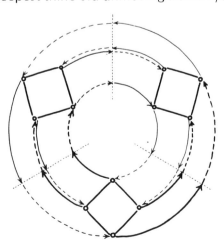

(Transition on the last line)

Vortakt A O T
Nachtakt T A O

Note: This piece is particularly suitable for Grade 7.

Michaelmas (II)
W. M. von Heider

Look up and behold
Stretched o'er the harvest gold,
Michael's sword of light.

Fed on our human fears
See how the dragon rears
Out of the depths of night.

Give us the Bread of Life
Strengthen us for the strife
Michael, Lord of Light.

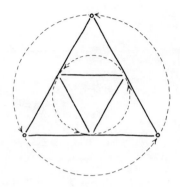

Verse for Michaelmas
Angelus Silesius

When I conquer within me fear and wrath,
Saint Michael in heaven casts the dragon forth.

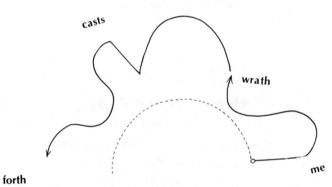

Behold the Plant
Friedrich Ruckert
freely translated by W.M. von Heider

Behold the plant within the seed
Enchanted form as yet unfreed.

Growth gently pushes root and shoot,
Forming leaves and flowers and fruit.

Gaily adorned with colors fair,
Ornamenting earth and air.

It develops, it unfolds
All that once its heart did hold.

Spanish Carol

Up now laggardly lasses,
Up awake and away,
Out and gone before cock-crow
On the road before day.
Mary meek and gentle,
Rose of Jericho,
Bore a babe and laid him
In a manger low.

Stand for last line

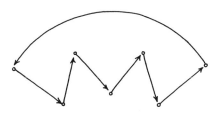

Carol

Christmas Eve

As up the wood I took my way, The oaks were brown and bare, And all about the snow was white, the snow was white, the snow was white, And all about the snow was white, And bitter blew the air.

As up the wood I took my way,
The oaks were brown and bare,
And all about the snow was white, (*repeat*)
And bitter blew the air.

As up the wood I took my way
The night began to fall,
When out a star shone fair and bright, (*repeat*)
And I heard a sweet voice call:

"Come on, come on, thou weary man,"
   The sweet voice cried to me,
"For in yon shed where the cattle are,
   I have good sight for thee."

Then suddenly grew the snow to rose,
The bare oaks grew to green,
The bitter wind was a gentle air, (*repeat*)
And I felt not fear nor teen.

For golden Gabriel took my hand
And brought me to the shed,
Where 'mid the cattle sat Queen Mary, (*repeat*)
And rocked Lord Jesus' bed.

Hie then good shepherds and masters mine,
We'll cease to moil and grieve,
For this brave babe is the Lord of all, (*repeat*)
And this is Christmas Eve.

Lorelei
Alexander Macmillan

I canna tell what has come ower me
   That I am sae eerie and wae;
An auld world tale comes before me,
   It haunts me by nicht and by day.

From the cool lift the gloamin' draps dimmer,
   And the Rhine slips saftly by;
The taps of the mountains shimmer
   I' the lowe o' the sunset sky.

Up there, in a glamor entrancin;
   Sits a maiden woundrous fair;
Her gowden adornments are glancing,
   She is kaimin' her gowden hair.

As she kaims it, the gowd kaim glistens,

The while she is singin' a song
That hauds the rapt soul that listens,
    With its melody sweet and strong.

The boy, floating by in vague wonder,
    Is seized with a wild weird love;
He sees na the black rocks under, —
    He sees but the vision above.

The waters their waves are flingin'
    Ower boatie and boatman anon;
And this, with her airtful singin',
    The Waterwitch Lurly hath done.

Continuous Form

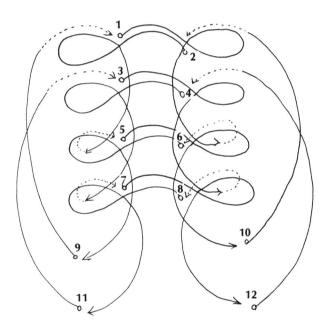

This form can also be used for "The White Birds" by W. B. Yeats.

The Ballad of Semmerwater
Sir William Watson

Deep asleep, deep asleep,
Deep asleep it lies,
The still lake of Semmerwater
Under the still skies.

And many a fathom, many a fathom,
Many a fathom below,
In a king's tower and a queen's bower
The fishes come and go.

Once there stood by Semmerwater,
A mickle town and tall,
King's tower and queen's bower
And the wakeman on the wall.

Came a beggar halt and sore;
"I faint for lack of bread,"
King's tower and queen's bower
Cast him forth unfed.

He knocked at the door of the herdsman's cot,
The herdsman's cot in the dale,
They gave him of their oatcake,
They gave him of their ale.

He has cursed aloud that city proud,
He has cursed it in its pride;
He has cursed it into Semmerwater
Down the brant hillside;
He has cursed it into Semmerwater,
There to bide.

King's tower and Queen's bower
And a mickle town and tall,
By glimmer of scale and gleam of fin,
Folk have seen them all.
King's tower and queen's bower
And weed and reed in the gloom,
And a lost city of Semmerwater
Deep asleep till doom.

The Temptation of Saint Anthony
French

Goblins came on mischief bent
To Saint Anthony in Lent.

Come ye goblins small and big,
We will kill the hermit's pig.

While the good monk minds his books,
We the hams will cure and cook.

While he goes down on his knees,
We will fry the sausages.

On his knees went Anthony
To those imps of Barbary.

Good kind goblins, spare his life,
He to me is child and wife.

He is my felicity,
Spare, o spare my pig to me.

But the pig they did not spare,
Did not heed the hermit's prayer.

While the good monk read his book,
They the hams did cure and cook.

Still he rose not from his knees,
While they fried the sausages.

All at once the morning broke,
From his dreams the monk awoke.

There in the kind light of day
Was the little pig at play.

The Common Cormorant
or Shag
Anonymous

The common cormorant or shag
Lays eggs inside a paper bag;
The reason you will see, no doubt,
It is to keep the lightning out.
But what these unobservant birds
Have never noticed is
That herds
Of wandering bears may
Come with buns
And steal the bags to hold the crumbs.

Who?
Anonymous

Out of his hole
To steal he stole,
His bag of chink he chunk,
And many a weary smile he smole
And many a wink he wunk.

Chapter Eight

High School, Grades Nine to Twelve (Ages Fourteen to Eighteen)

Little is gained by noting down the main lesson subjects in high school. On the one hand, many new subjects are introduced; on the other hand, some subjects appear to be a recapitulation of previous periods. For instance, in Grades 9 and 10, in history of art and literature classes, pupils become aware of the changing consciousness of man from pre-Christian to modern times. In Grades 5 and 6, they learnt through legends and the first records of history how man became more and more attached to the earth and more and more skilful in the use of its resources. Now they are able to understand the change from the old dependence on tribal laws and patterns of life based on the blood bond to the newer conception of individual freedom and world brotherhood.*

Newcomers to Eurythmy

Pupils who have never done Eurythmy are often admitted in the middle or upper school. Should these new pupils sit out and watch the lesson? Should they, for instance, learn the intervals if they have not learnt the notes of the scale? Should they learn the soul-gestures if they have not learnt the movements for the vowels and consonants?

It can also happen that a class has not had Eurythmy for several years. Should the Eurythmist begin where the children left off three years ago? The question is often asked, "Should I begin at the beginning with the children?"

There is no one answer. If it is possible for the Eurythmist to give these newcomers extra help, it is always best to begin with the exercises that are right for that particular age group. For instance, the twelve-year-olds should learn the intervals first and then go on to learn major and minor chords, scales, and so on. There are so many approaches to Eurythmy. The exercises for the age group can be a beginning, and there will always be part of the lesson in which the newcomers can join—for instance, concentration exercises, rhythms, or beat.

Pupils should never "copy" the movements for the vowels and consonants without knowing what they are doing. Sometimes classmates will offer to teach a newcomer how to do a concentration exercise or a rod exercise. This usually works well. If there are only one or two new pupils in a class, they usually manage to fit in and catch up, especially if all the children in the class are learning something that is new to everyone.

---

*The curriculum of the first Waldorf School, assembled by C. von Heydebrand, with the supplement on English and English literature by Eileen Hutchins M.A., is a concise and helpful guide for Eurythmy teachers. Also helpful is *Rudolf Steiner's Curriculum for the Waldorf Schools* by E. A. Karl Stockmeyer. Both books are published by the Rudolf Steiner Press, 35 Park Road, London, England.

Eurythmy with Grades Nine to Twelve

Girl in Grade 9: "When I'm doing Eurythmy, I know what it is, but when my Aunty asks me to explain it, I don't know what to say. What do you say when people ask you what Eurythmy is?"

By the end of Grade 8, the foundation will have been laid for all the elements of Eurythmy. In high school there can be a more individual relationship between pupil and teacher. This and the young person's growing ability to think and reason demand a different approach to Eurythmy. It becomes increasingly evident that the pupils are beginning to think for themselves and consequently they also question their work and their teachers. They will undoubtedly want to know more about Eurythmy, why it is not taught in other schools, and what it is.

The young people should be taken seriously; they should be given an opportunity to talk with their teacher about this new art. They should not stand around in the Eurythmy room as if interrupting the lesson, but meet in their own classroom. They should never be fobbed off with such phrases as "because it is good for you." It is an opportunity that should not be missed. Not only the art of Eurythmy but also the therapeutic work and remedial Eurythmy can be discussed. There is more inborn understanding of Eurythmy today among young people than ever before.

It is also true that there are always a few "disturbers," especially in Grade 9, and these disturbers usually have the loudest voices even though they are in the minority. There is often a tendency only to hear and occupy oneself with them, while the really interested are forgotten. If certain pupils disturb Eurythmy lessons, Rudolf Steiner said they should be given the task of drawing movement, for instance the movement of the rod in the rod exercises. This should not be given as punishment but as a different task. These pupils should be told to bring paper, pencils, compasses, and rulers to the next lesson. They should watch the exercise carefully once. The second time it could be done very slowly and then they could draw it while the rest of the class continues practising. Geometrical forms such as inversions and rotations could also be drawn.

In fact, it is a good idea to keep Eurythmy notebooks from about Grade 4 or 5 on. The children can write the poems they learn and draw the forms with colored pencils. If this is done regularly throughout the school years, maybe there will not be any disturbers in Grade 9.

In high school a new approach can be made through color and form. The consonants and vowels and exercises such as contraction and expansion and forms of symmetry can be experienced at a different level. Poems should be chosen in connection with the literature and art being studied. The Eurythmist, as always, must work closely in cooperation with the other teachers. Different styles can be practiced for German, French, and English Eurythmy; also for the history of art period for Indian, Egyptian, Greek, and Norse poetry.

Thinking, feeling, and willing forms are experienced together with epic, lyrical, and dramatic poetry. The expressions for similes, metaphors, and various verse forms are practiced in Eurythmy.

Certain forms given by Dr. Steiner may be practiced in high school, such as, "The Wonder at the Spring" from the second Mystery Play.* The form for "Wie herrlich leuchtet mir die Natur" can be used with a similar English lyric of four lines. There are also forms for Goethe's "An die Natur" and Fercher von Steinwand's "Die Urtriebe." The *Auftakte* forms (Merry Measure, Elegy, Mood of Nature, Tiaoait, Cosmic Auftakt, and so on) can also be practiced during this year.

The Soul's Probation, Scene 5, by Rudolf Steiner, Steiner Book Center, Toronto.

All these forms are healing and harmonizing. It is good to know this and realize that the forms work powerfully.

In Grades 11 and 12, the pupils are led to experience the relationship of the vowel sounds with the planets, and the relationship of the consonants with the Zodiac Gestures. In Grade 12, apart from group forms, the Eurythmist should work with individual students and help them prepare and practice poetry and music that they themselves have chosen.

Many questions have been raised and left unanswered in these notes on Eurythmy with older students. Throughout their lives, Eurythmists will need to seek a way of answering these. They will also need to continue to seek new ways of teaching Eurythmy so that an awareness of the etheric world can be awakened.

In the future much will depend on this awareness in humanity.

Useful Alliterations

from **The Vision of Piers Plowman**
William Langland

On a May morning   on the Malvern Hills
A marvel befell me   of fairy methought,
Thus I went wide   where walking alone,
In a wide wilderness   by a woodside,
Bliss of the birds' song   made me abide there,
And on a lawn under a linden   I leaned awhile
To listen to their lays   their lovely notes,
The mirth of their mouths   made me to muse
And mid that bliss   I dreamed marvelously.

Christmas Carol
Fifteenth Century

I saw a sweet and simple sight,
A blissful bride, a blossom bright
That morning made and mirth among
A maiden mother meek and mild
In cradle kept a newborn child
That softly slept; she sat and sang
Lullay, lullow, lully, lully, lully
    Lully, lully, lully, lully,
Lullow Lully, lullay, baw, baw,
My bairn, sleep softly now.

Ragnarok*
Eileen Hutchins

Behold, there breaketh
The day of doom,
Darkness descendeth,
The elements rage.
Thunder rolls loud
And lightnings flash fire,
Earth splits asunder,
Heaven falls in flames.

Take courage, my heroes,
Now as of old,
Let mood be the mightiest
Blood burn with fire.
Rend, o ye Norns,
Your weaving of runes,
The gods great ending
Dawneth at last.

Through the stress of the storm,
Through the darkness of death,
There flashes the flame
Of fire through the night.
Behold in his beauty
There riseth once more
A God in his glory
Of love and of light.

---

*Eurythmy forms for the first and last verses only.

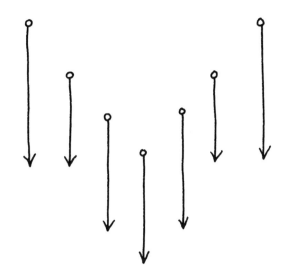

"Behold, there breaketh
The day of doom"

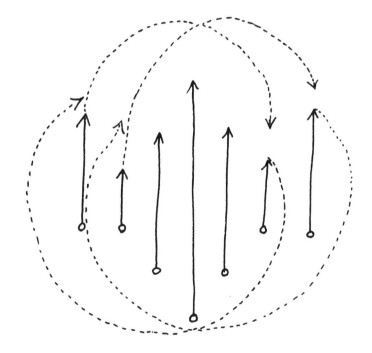

"Darkness descendeth,
The elements rage.

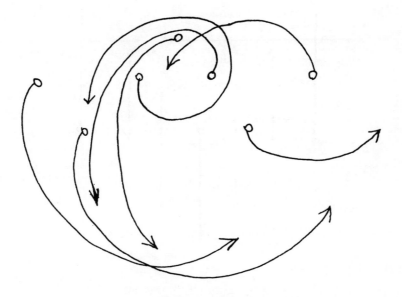

Thunder rolls loud"

"And lightnings flash fire,

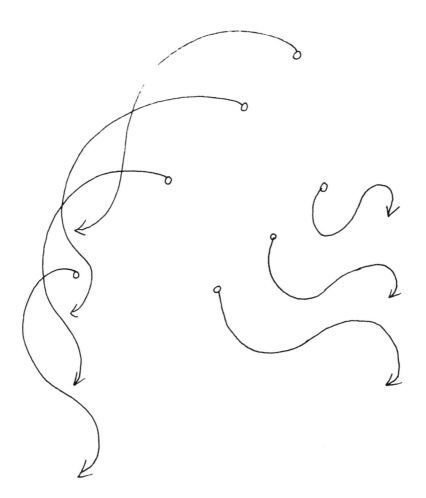

Earth splits asunder,

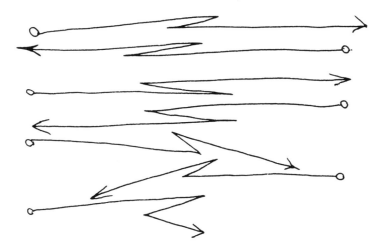

Heaven falls in flames."

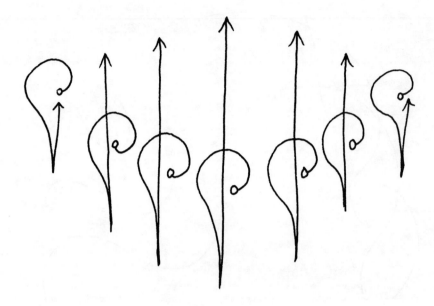

"Through the stress of the storm,
Through the darkness of death,

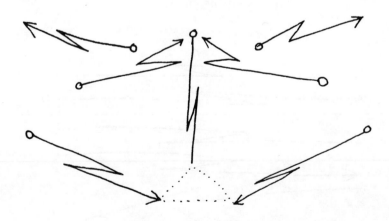

There flashes the flame"

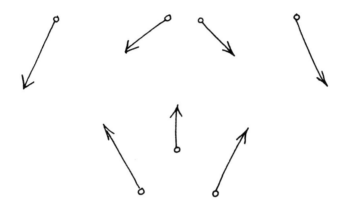

"Of fire through the night."

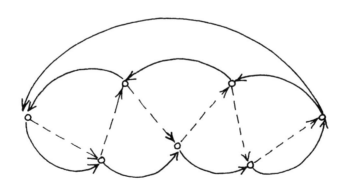

"Behold in his beauty
There riseth once more"

(Standing; one step back on "riseth" — future zone into present zone.)

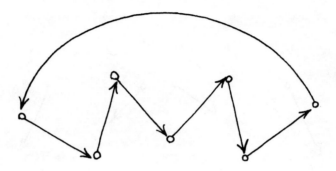

"A God in his glory"

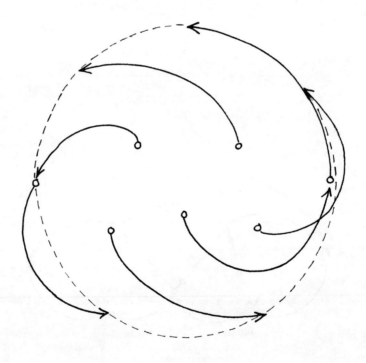

"Of Love and of light."

Dame Death
Medieval

She was grisly and great and grim to behold,
The foulest freak that formed was ever,
Both of hide and of hue and of hair also.
She was long and lean and lodly to see;
There was no man on the mould so mighty of strength
But a look of that Lady and his life passed.
Her eyes farden as the fire that in the furnace burns,
They were hollow in her head with heavy brows.
Her cheeks were lean, with lips full side
With a marvelous mouth full of long tushes.
Her lere, like the lead that latest was beaten.
She bare in her right hand an unrid weapon
And bright burnished blade all bloody beronnen;
And in the left hand, like the leg of a grype,
With talents that were touching and teenful enough.
With that she burnished up her band and bradde out her gear.
And I, for fear of that freake, fell in a swoud.

Dame Life
Medieval

Shee was brighter of her blee,[1]
    Then was the bright sonn:
Her rudd[2] redder than the rose,
    That on the rise hangeth:
Meekly smiling with her mouth,
    And merry in her lookes.
Ever laughing for love,
    As shee like would.
And as shee came by the bankes,
    The boughs eche one
They louted to that ladye
    And layd forth their branches;
Blossomes, and burgens
    Breathed full sweete;
Flowers flourished in the frith[3]
    Where shee forth stepped;
And the grasse, that was gray,
    Greened believe.[4]

[1]Being.   [2]Complexion.   [3]Woods.   [4]At once.

Christmas
Anonymous

The eternal light it shines in here,   **Expansion**
It makes the world so bright and clear,
It bans the darkness of the night   **Contraction**
And makes us children of the light.   **Expansion**

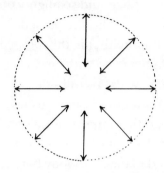

Ave Maris Stella

Ave maris stella,   **1st Verse**
   The star on the sea,   **Latin. . . straight lines**
Dei mater alma,   **English. . .curve to next place**
   Blessed mot [may] she be,   **last line to center**
Atque semper virgo,
   Pray thy son for me,
Felix caeli porta,
   That I may come to thee.

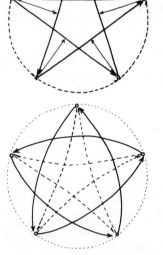

Gabriel that archangel,
   He was messenger;
So fair he gret our Lady
   With an "ave" so clear:
"Hail be thou, Mary,
   Be thou, Mary,
Full of Goddes grace,
   And Queen of Mercy."

from **Hymn of the Nativity**
Richard Crashaw

Welcome, all wonders in one sight!
   Eternity shut in a span.
Summer in winter, day in night,
   Heaven in earth, and God in man!   **Spirals or contraction and**
Great little one! whose all-embracing birth   **expansion.**
   Lifts earth to heaven, stoops heaven to earth.

Isaiah IX: Verses 2-6

The people that walked in darkness
Have seen a great light:

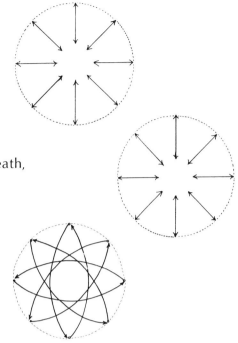

And they that dwell in the Land of the shadow of death,
Upon them hath the light shined.

For unto us a child is born,
Unto us a son is given!

And the government shall be upon his shoulder;

And his name shall be called Wonderful, Counsellor,
The Mighty God, the Everlasting Father,
The Prince of Peace.

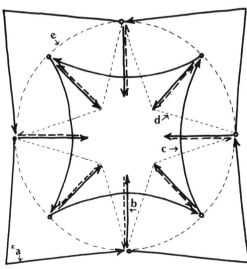

The government . . . . a (all)	**The mighty god** . . . . e (1st group)
And his name . . . . b (all)	**The everlasting father** . a (2nd group)
Wonderfull . . . . c (1st group)	**The Prince of Peace** . . . . b (all)
Councellor . . . . d (2nd group)	

Verse
Rudolf Steiner

The light of the sun gives strength to all things on earth.
The sunlight of truth gives strength to the human heart.

Space
Angelus Silesius

Thou art not set in space,
But space is set in thee,
If thou wilt cast it out,
Thou hast eternity.

God Is as Small as I
Angelus Silesius

God is as small as I,
I am as great as He;
I am not under Him,
He is not over me.

from Nature
**Johann Wolfgang von Goethe,
translated by W. M. von Heider**

(1)   O Nature! She surrounds and enfolds us.   **Doctor Form.**

(2)   We are powerless to withdraw and powerless to enter more deeply into her
        being.

(3)   Unbidden and unwarned she whirls us into the cycle of her dance until we
        are weary and sink from her arms.

(3–4) She is forever creating fresh forms. Everything is new, yet always old.

(4–5) She is forever building and destroying. She lives in countless children but
        their Mother, where is she?   **Silently into 3.**

(3-4) She is the unique artist. She is performing a play.   **Silently into 2.**

(2-3) There is an everlasting life and growth in her. She transforms herself
        ceaselessly.   **Into 1.**

(1-2) She is never a moment still.
      Her step is measured,

(2-1) Her exceptions rare,
      Her laws immutable.   **Silently into 5.**

(5-6) She has thought
      And still she ponders.

(6-7) We are all living in her and she lives in each of us.   **Into 5.**

(5-6) Even the most unnatural is nature,
      Even the crudest and commonest are tinged with her genius.   **Silently into 4.**

(4-5) She loves herself,
      She delights in illusions,

(5-6) She showers her creations forth from the void.

(6-7) Life is her finest invention,
      Death her masterpiece,   **Silently into 2.**

(2-3) Whereby she achieves abundant life.   **Silently into 1.**

To Sea, To Sea!

from **"Songs from 'Death's Jestbook'"**
Thomas Lovell Beddoes

To sea, to sea! The calm is o'er;   Form for rhythm.
The wanton water leaps in sport,
And rattles down the pebbly shore;
The dolphin wheels, the sea-cows snort,
And unseen Mermaids' pearly song
Comes bubbling up, the weeds among.
    Fling broad the sail, dip deep the oar:
To sea, to sea! the calm is o'er.

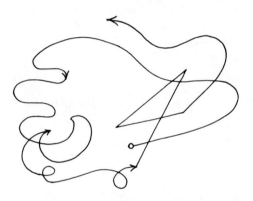

To sea, to sea! our wide-wing'd bark
Shall billowy cleave its sunny way,
And with its shadow, fleet and dark,
Break the cav'd Tritons' azure day,
Like mighty eagle soaring light
O'er antelopes on Alpine height.
    The anchor heaves, the ship swings free,
The sails swell full. To sea, to sea!

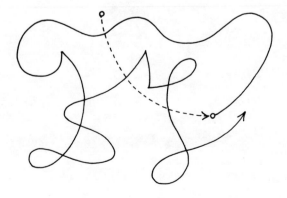

Happy
Merry Measure

Oh, I am as happy as a big sunflower
That nods and bends in the breezes!
And my heart is as light as the wind that blows
The leaves from off the treeses!

Old Rhyme
Merry Measure

Merry are the bells and merry would they ring,
Merry was myself and merry could I sing;
With a merry ding dong, happy, gay, and free
And a merry sing song, happy let us be!

Merry have we met and merry have we been,
Merry let us part and merry meet again,
With a merry sing song, happy, gay, and free
With a merry ding dong, happy let us be.

Old Song*

I was once young upon a day,
Oh I was once young upon a day
I was wandering all alone.
I was wandering all alone.

Glad was I when I met another,
Oh, glad was I when I met another,
For man is the joy of man.
Man is the joy of man.

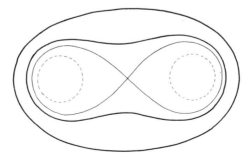

*The **words** of the High One from the *Elder Edda* are very similar.

My Heart Leaps Up

William Wordsworth

My heart leaps up when I behold
A rainbow in the sky:
So was it when my life began;
So is it now I am a man;
So be it when I shall grow old,
Or let me die!
The Child is Father of the Man;
And I could wish my days to be
Bound each to each by natural piety.

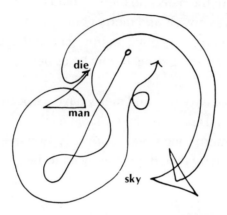

Thinking, feeling, and willing forms.

Pack, Clouds, Away

from "The Rape of Lucrece"
Thomas Heywood

Pack, clouds, away, and welcome day!
   With night we banish sorrow.
Sweet air, blow soft; mount, lark, aloft
   To give my love good morrow.
Wings from the wind to please her mind,
   Notes from the lark I'll borrow:
Bird, prune thy wing, nightingale, sing,
   To give my love good morrow.
     To give my love good morrow,
     Notes from them all I'll borrow.

Wake from thy nest, robin redbreast!
   Sing, birds, in every furrow,
And from each bill let music shrill
   Give my fair love good morrow.
Blackbird and thrush in every bush,

Stare, linnet, and cock-sparrow,
You pretty elves, amongst yourselves
Sing my fair love good morrow.
To give my love good morrow,
Sing, birds, in every furrow.*

The Spring

Thomas Carew

Now that the winter's gone, the earth has lost
Her snow-white robes; and now no more the frost
Candies the grass, or casts an icy cream
Upon the silver lake or crystal stream:

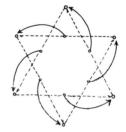

But the warm sun thaws the benumbed earth,
And makes it tender; gives a second birth
To the dead swallow, wakes in hollow tree
The drowsy cuckoo and the humble bee.

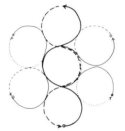

Now do a choir of chirping minstrels sing,
In triumph to the world, the youthful Spring,
The valleys, hills, and woods in rich array
Welcome the coming of the long'd-for May.

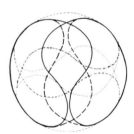

*Note: If there are eight participants the second verse can be done as a canon on an octagon.

Vernal Equinox

Sol revenit,
Terra ridet,
Per tenebras
Lucem videt.

Forms based on vowel sounds. This verse could also be done with contraction and expansion.

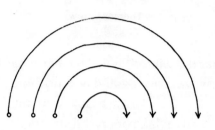

"Sol revenit,"

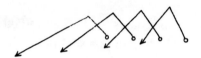

"Terra ridet"

"Per tenebras"

"Lucem videt."

Adoration of the Disk
from "**The Book of the Dead**"
Ancient Egyptian,
translated by Robert Hillyer

Thy dawn, O Ra, opens the new horizon,   **Cosmic Measure**
and every realm that thou hast made to live
Is conquered by thy love, as joyous day
Follows thy footsteps in delightful peace.

And when thou settest, all the world is bleak;
Houses are tombs where blind men lie in death;
Only the lion and the serpent move
Through the black oven of the sightless night.

Dawn in the East again! the lands awake,
Men leap from their slumber with a song;
They bathe their bodies, clothe them in fresh garments,
And lift their hands in happy adoration.

Sun
from **The Sun Dances**   **Gaelic**

The eye of the great God,   **The Cosmic Measure**
The eye of the God of glory,
The eye of the King of hosts,
The eye of the King of the living,
Pouring upon us
At each time and season,
Pouring upon us
Gently and generously.

Glory to thee,
Thou glorious sun.

Glory to thee, thou sun,
Face of the God of life.

The Planets
from Faust, **Part 2, Act 1**
Johann Wolfgang von Goethe

Harken, Hark! The hours careering   **Venus, Sun, Mercury**
Sounding loud to spirit hearing,   **Sun, Mercury**

See the newborn day appearing.	**Mercury, Saturn, Jupiter, Mars, Mercury**
Thundering the light streams near,	**Moon, Mercury**
Pealing rays and trumpet blazes,	**Mercury, Mars**
Eye is blinded, ear amazes,	**Moon, Mercury, Mars**
The unheard can no one hear.	**Mercury, Jupiter, Mercury**

Eurythmy Forms

Continuous Forms

These can be used either as *Auftakte* with sounds such as LA, LO or as a basic form for poems.

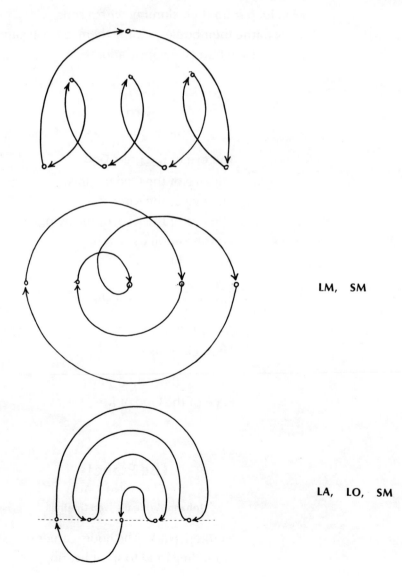

LM,   SM

LA,   LO,   SM

This form is based on the maze at Boughton Green.

The maze could be formed by pupils moving swiftly and silently following a leader. As a canon: When 1 is at 2, II begins; when I is at 3, II is at 2 and III begins.

The meeting points are also turning points—points of social consciousness that could be marked by a clash of cymbals. The maze could also be formed by pairs of pupils to make a labyrinth.

Exercise for Vowels and Diphthongs

F. Thomas Simons

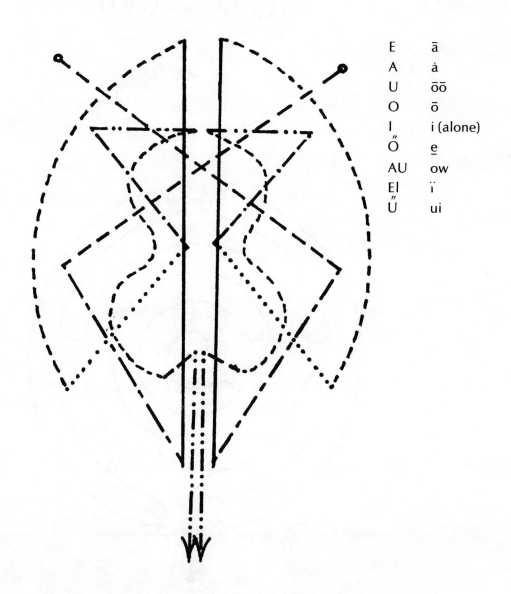

E	ā
A	à
U	ōō
O	ō
I	i (alone)
Ő	e̲
AU	ow
EI	ï
Ű	ui

In this exercise the vowel sound is formed between the partners; for example, E—each one forms the sound with the outside arm only (Uōō with the inside arm).

The Evolutionary Sequence

F. Thomas Simons

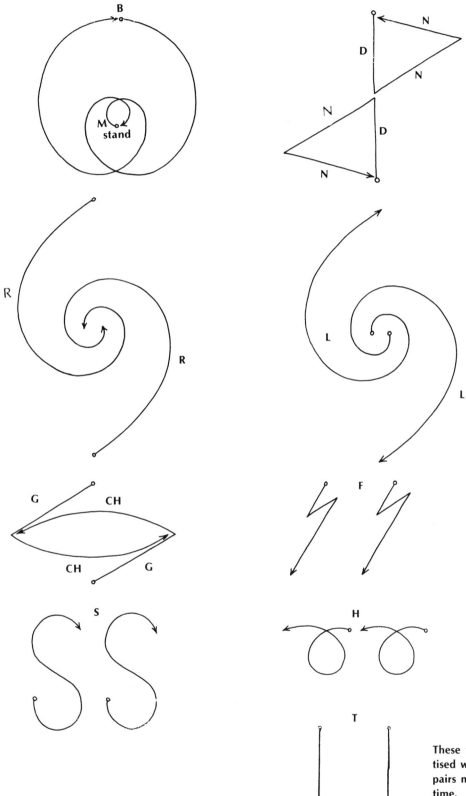

These forms can be practised with any number of pairs moving at the same time.

Play

Midsummer Eve

Eileen Hutchins

Cast of Characters

Robin	**Fair Ellen**
Elfin Queen	**Demons**
Elves	**Chorus**

CHORUS: It was the Eve of Midsummer
When all the world was gay
And men and maids came out to dance
About the close of day.

O make for us a song, Robin!
O pipe for us a tune!
That we may dance a fair new dance
Upon this night of June!

ROBIN: If I am to make some merry music
For dancing in the ring,
I must go alone to the wild green glade
And hear how the birds do sing!

CHORUS: O, do not go to the glade, Robin,
Where the broom is gold and fair,
For the Elfin Queen will pass that way
And hold you in her snare.
O do not go to the glade, Robin,
Where the broom is gold and gay,
For the elves will draw you to their dance
And hold you for ever and aye.

ROBIN: O what care I for the Elfin Queen?
O what care I for the dance?
There I shall hear a sweeter music
Than ever on earth will chance.

FAIR ELLEN: Remember then, O Robin,
Your troth to me you plight,
That you and I would lead the dance
And leap the fire tonight.

ROBIN: I'll keep my promise, fair Ellen,
              My troth to you I plight,
              That we shall lead the Midsummer dance
              And leap the fire tonight.

CHORUS: He goes alone to the haunted glade
              Where the winds so softly blow;
              The sweet birds sing in the leafy wood
              And the waters murmur low.

              He hears a sweeter music
              Than ever on earth he heard;
              It is sweeter far than the skylark's note
              Or the song of the throstle bird.

              The Elfin Queen comes by that way,
              She greets him with delight.
              "O Robin, if you would learn our song
              Come dance with me tonight."

              She takes him into the Elfin ring;
              The moon shines pale and fair,
              She casts her magic spell on him
              To dance forever there.

              (On the village green)

CHORUS: The maids are all arrayed with flowers,
              The fairest ever seen.
              The men are in their gay attire
              To dance upon the green.

              But where is our minstrel Robin?
              They call him far and wide.
              He does not come to lead the dance
              This fair Midsummer tide.
              Then up and speaks fair Ellen,

FAIR ELLEN: His vow to me he made,
              And I must go to win him back
              From out the haunted glade.

CHORUS: The wind grows cold and the clouds are dark,

The moon shines pale and chill;
Fair Ellen leaves the merry throng
And climbs the lonely hill.

Among the thorns and the thistles sharp,
Behind the rocks so grim,
The demons of the night come creeping
Out of the shadows dim.
They hear fair Ellen coming,
They giggle and grimace.

DEMONS: No human maid shall pass this way
To the enchanted place.

Let's beat her hence with briars,
Let's tear her flesh with thorns.
She'll never dare to come again
For many nights and morns.

CHORUS: They beat her brow with briars,
They pierce her to the bone;
The bitter thorns draw forth her blood,
But still she makes no moan.

She passes through their power
To the enchanted glade,
She stands before the Elfin Queen
And meets her unafraid.

FAIR ELLEN: I come to claim my lover
And win him back from you,
For he has made his vow to me
And now must prove it true.

ELFIN QUEEN: I do not give you back your love
Because he gave his troth;
Men's promises are like the wind
And little are they worth.

But you have faced the darksome night
And borne the bitter pain.
Your power is mightier than mine
To win him back again.

And Robin for your true love's sake,
And as you've danced with me,
You still shall remember our Elfin songs
And recall our minstrelsy.

I lay my finger on your lips
My hand upon your heart;
You shall be the teller of magic tales
And know our secret art.

CHORUS: Now as they leave the haunted glade
About the midnight hour,
The demons hide in the deepest shade
Their spells have lost their power.

And when they reach the village green,
There's many a loud "Hooray!
Why, Robin, welcome back again,
Three years you've been away."

Now Robin plays upon his pipe,
The magical refrain;
He leads fair Ellen to the dance,
And all is joy again.

(Country dance.)

This play can be performed by several classes. Robin, Ellen, and the chorus of country folk are the actors. The demons, the Elfin Queen, and her elves do Eurythmy.

Four Medieval Verses For Teachers

The Stumbling Block
from The Statues of Nuns
German

Lightly and gaily the sanguine skips over the stumbling block.
If he trips, he cares not, it hinders him hardly at all.

Grimly the choleric kicks at the block hurling it out of his way.
As he exults in his strength, see how his eye flashes fire.

When the phlegmatic appears, he pensively slows down his step,
"If this block will not move from my path, I shall have to go round it, that's all."

Now by the block the melancholic is brooding and sunk in despair,
"My footsteps are dogged by bad luck, such things always happen to me!"

The verses mirror the reaction of each temperament when confronted with the stumbling block that life invariably lays at our feet.

Appendix

Advice and Indications
Given by Dr. Steiner for Eurythmy*

The following fundamental advice was given by Dr. Steiner to Eurythmy teachers: "Begin the lesson earnestly, finish merrily. In this way the sediment accumulated in the body by sitting in previous lessons can be completely dispersed during the merry half of the eurythmy class and the children will then be receptive for the next lessons."

In the brief indications listed below Dr. Steiner points out the specific value of each exercise.

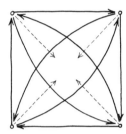

> Wir suchen uns,
> Wir leben uns
> Ganz nah.

This exercise develops the ability to orientate oneself quickly in any circumstance—versatility. The usual translation of the verse is:

> We seek one another
> We feel one another
> Quite near.

It is, however, important to keep the vowel sounds I (e) E (a) A (a); they are an essential part of the form experience, therefore I suggest something like the following:

> We will seek you—
> We're aware of you—
> There you are!

The Harmonious Eight
fosters inner harmony.

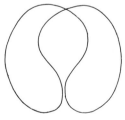

---

*From Anregungen fur den Eurythmie-Unterricht von Nora von Baditz, Uitgeverij Vrij Geestesleven, Tesselschadelaan 7-Zeist-Holland

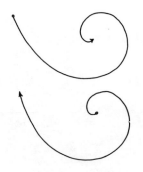

Question and Answer: "Furthers intelligence and awakens strength and initiative for one's own work."

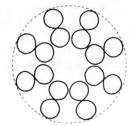

The Little Eights in the Big Circle "Dance of Planets." "Wakens a feeling for the whole of humanity.

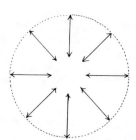

Contraction and Expansion "furthers intelligence and initiative."

Tiaoait is an "exercise to correct tangled thinking— brings order into thinking."

Apollonian Forms "harmonise thinking, feeling, and willing."

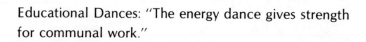

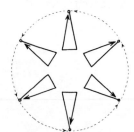

Educational Dances: "The energy dance gives strength for communal work."

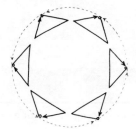

The Peace Dance is an "entering into the mood of peace."

I and You are We "counteracts vanity, ambition and egoism." (Dr. Steiner explains that a certain danger lies in these three characteristics which could lead to mental illness.)

Dr. Steiner gave permission to use the four archetypal movements of the Zodiac in educational Eurythmy—Taurus, Leo, Scorpio, and Aquarius—so that young people could experience the strength of the moral world order. These gestures precede and follow the exercise which is done by four people.

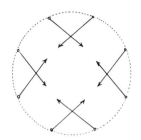

"You and I are Struggling Fiercely with Each Other" This has a very calming effect on children. "Their being is completely absorbed by this activity."

For unintelligent children it is good to move from an irregular arrangement during a poem or roundelay into a regular form.

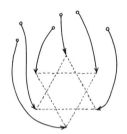

Here We Are expresses "the joy of being together."

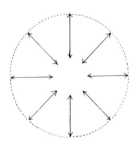

The Rod Exercises "Correct waywardness in posture." "Gegen die Ungezogenheiten der Korperhaltung."

Continuous Eights "foster healthy joyfulness."

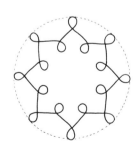

Spirals that curve in are "good for pale or anaemic children."

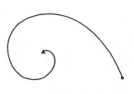

Spirals that curve out are "good for plethoric (vollblutige) or egoistical children."

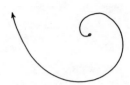

Moving without a pause from straight lines into curved forms develops new etheric forces.

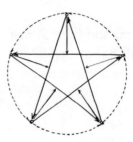
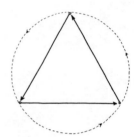

"It is refreshing to practise certain exercises slowly getting quicker and quickly getting slower."

Der Wolkendurchleuchter "has a calming effect."

Here is a free rendering from the German:

He who illumines the clouds
May He illumine
May He shine through
May He glow through
May He warm through and through
Even me.

"In Eurythmy the experience must always precede the gesture."

Certain geometrical forms that can be arranged in the circle "are good to wake children up."

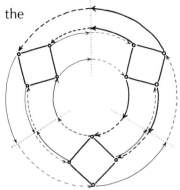

I (e): this sound must always be done with joy.

The calming consonants are D F G K H.
The stimulating consonants are L M N P Q.
"Tired despondent pupils will wake up and become interested." (R keeps the balance between the calming and stimulating consonants).

The protecting consonants are V B S T.

"If a person has difficulty in speaking R a certain harmony is lacking in his being. Practise frequently R in Eurythmy."

Quotations from Dr. Steiner

In response to a teacher who spoke about children who are not good at arithmetic: "If you discover a special weakness in arithmetic it will be good to do as follows: as a rule the other children will have two gymnastic lessons in the week, or rather one Eurythmy lesson and one gymnastic lesson. You can make a group of children who are not good at arithmetic and let them have an extra hour or half-hour of Eurythmy or gymnastics. This need not mean a lot of extra work for you: you can take them with others who are doing the same kind of exercises, but you must try to improve these children's capacities by means of Gymnastics and Eurythmy. First give them rod exercises; tell them: "Hold the rod in your hand, first in front counting 1,2,3; then behind 1,2,3,4." Each time the child must change the position of the rod, moving it from front to back. He must make a great effort in some way to get the rod behind him at 3. Then add walking, say, 3 steps forwards, 5 steps backwards; 3 steps forwards, 4 steps backwards; 5 steps forwards, 3 steps backwards and so on. Try in Gymnastics and also perhaps in Eurythmy to combine number with the child's movements, so that he is obliged to count while he is moving. You will find that this has an effect. I have frequently done this with pupils.

A teacher said: Eurythmy movements must be a great help in the teaching of Geometry:

"But I did not mean geometry. What I said applied to arithmetic because what lies at the root of arithmetic is consciously willed movement, the sense of movement. When you bring the sense of movement into activity in this way you will quicken a child's arithmetical powers. You bring something up out of the subconscious which in such a child is not willing to be brought up. Speaking generally, if a child is bad both at arithmetic and geometry this should be remedied by exercises in movement. You will be able to do a great deal for a child's progress in geometry with varied and inventive Eurythmy exercises, and rod exercises also."*

On the subject of children who do not want to do Eurythmy:

"With regard to the children who do not want to do Eurythmy there is yet another way of bringing them to take pleasure in it. Besides letting them frequently watch Eurythmy, try to take photographs of various Eurythmy positions. These must be simplified so that the child will get visual images of Eurythmic forms and movements made by the human being. Pictures of this kind will make an impres-

---

*From the Eighth Discussion, *Discussions with Teachers*, Rudolf Steiner Press, London.

sion on the children and will kindle their Eurythmic ability. . . . I don't mean simply reproductions of Eurythmic positions but transformed into simple patterns of movement which have an artistic effect. These could be used to show the children the beauty of line. You would then discover an extraordinarily interesting psychological fact, that the child could perceive the beauty of line which he has himself produced in Eurythmy without becoming vain and coquettish. Whereas otherwise he is liable to become vain if his attention is drawn to what he has done himself, in Eurythmy this is obviated. So that in Eurythmy also you can cultivate a perception of line that can be used to enhance the feeling of self without awakening vanity and coquettishness."*

On Rhythm:

Now you will understand why it is that when a child first starts going to school he is more likely to have an understanding of melody than of harmony. Naturally this must not be taken pedantically. Pedantry must never be allowed to play a part in matters of art. Of course all sorts of things can be brought to the attention of the child. But just as he should really only understand the fifth during the first few years of school, and at the most the fourth as well, but not the third (which he does not begin to understand inwardly until his ninth year), so we can also say that he easily understands the element of melody but does not begin to comprehend harmony until his ninth or tenth year. The child understands tone of course, but the harmony connected with it can only be cultivated from that age on. The rhythmic element assumes the most varied forms. And the child will already understand a certain inner rhythm while he is still very young. But apart from the kind of rhythm thus experienced instinctively, the child should not be bothered with rhythm, as it is experienced for instance in instrumental music, until he is nine years old. That is when the child's attention should be drawn to these things. So in musical matters too it is possible to gather from the child's age what should be done. Approximately the same life-stages will be discovered here as in other fields in the theory and practice of Waldorf School education.**

---

*From the Eighth Discussion, *Discussions with Teachers*, Rudolf Steiner Press, London.

**From *Art in the Light of Wisdom*, Lecture 2, "The Realization of Tone in the Human Being," Rudolf Steiner Press, London.

English Eurythmy

Geographical conditions influence the plant kingdom. Geographical conditions also influence a language. Not only Americans, Australians, and South Africans have their particular way of speaking English, the people in the North, South, East, and West and Midlands of England have their individual pronounciation too. There are also many words that sound the same but have different spellings and meanings. How does the Eurythmist solve these problems?

It is obvious from Frau Neuscheller's notes that some of the indications given correspond to the American rather than to the English way of pronounciation. It is also important to note that not only the sound but also the spelling is at times taken into account. These indications seem to point to the written vowel (if it is in the root of the word) as the beginning of a movement that should flow swiftly into the movement for the audible vowel sound; for example,

castle (South of England)   A (ah)
castle (North of England)   A (ah) into a

(a) *sun*   (b) *son*

(a) If U (ōō) is in the root of the word but sounds A (ah) move swiftly from U to A (ah)
(b) If 0 is in the root of the word but sounds A (ah) move swiftly from O to A (ah)

The tendency today is toward phonetics, but the life and origin of a word is often retained in the spelling. Eurythmy can help us to develop a delicate sense for the being and life of the language.

The following notes are an attempt to summarize the various indications given to Eurythmists for English Eurythmy.

Vowels

German	English	
A	ar	As in spark, dark.
		A (ar) becomes R.
		Give the A (ar) over into the movement of the air.
	A	As in cap, man as ä.
		The movement can also be more open like the position
		for Aquarius.
		"Man, man, where will you land
		If you go on building on sand, on sand?"
E	a	Long as in Hail, gray.
		E (a) gently resounding into I (e)
		"Wait at the gate at break of day."

E	e	Short as in get, let.

E   e   Short as in get, let.
Short strong movement only with the wrists;
a quick, sharp knocking together.
    "Get in step, then wed."

I   e   Short as in if, stick.
Short pushing I (e)
    "It bit the little kitten."

IU   u   As in new, grandeur.
I (e) flowing into U (oo)
    "Dew fell pure and beautiful."

O   o   As in grow.
O (o) flowing into U (oo)
    "Over the rolling ocean."

O   a   As in God (American Let O resound into A).
Open O (English)
    "It is hot at the top."

O (or)   As in short, Law.
Open O with A character.
    "The glory of the dawn."

O (u)   As in color, son.
Short O A (ah). The A (ah) slightly held back.
    "I wonder, I wonder, will my love come."

O (er)   As in word and world.
When O is in the root of the word form the O consciously then dissolve it in ö (er)

Ö (er)   As in curl, heard, girl.
    "I turned and heard a bird sing in a fir tree."

U (u)   Short as in cut.
When U is in the root of the word from U (oo) into A
(ah) the A (ah) slightly held back.
    "The sun is out.
    run, run, have fun."

UI   As in quick, sweet.
Heavy U (oo) flowing into I (e) or Ü
    "The queen sang sweetly."

Oy   As in boy, enjoy.
Oi not eu
    "Little boy,
    full of joy."

EI   I   As in wide, life.
ai (ah)(e)
    "Kites fly
    high in the sky."

The Personal Pronoun I

Dr. Steiner gave the following indications: "On the one hand the English experience I, the ego, as the body, on the other hand the English experience themselves with their I, their ego in the physical surroundings, the environment. Therefore, 'I' is done as a movement of the whole body with Ai not Ei."

The "I" movement can be done like a spiral from within outward or from outside coming in. The head should be relaxed and accompany the movement. The 'I' movement done thus gives the experience of linking oneself with the world or the world with oneself.

Consonants

L	Silent as in walk, talk. Indicate I (e) with a slight stretching after an open O. Palm: an inner stretching into an A.	**(fiora, flora)** **(Firenza, Florence)**
GH	Silent as in caught, light. An expansion and indicate h.	
GH	As f as in laugh, rough. Do f and perhaps even add an h.	
K	Silent as knight, knife. Leave silent.	
W	Double U (oo). Heavy U (oo) from below upward, arms parallel.	
CH	As in chink, enchanter. Hold T downward until it explodes upwards in Sch; CH can also be done with a downward jump in T and dissolve in Sch. (T to the earth not on the head.)	
J or G	As in judge, German, joy. Indicate D before Sch; d hovering almost at the same time as sch; a generous movement.	
Th	This is obviously a very versatile sound, there are many indications.	
Th	*Voiceless* earth, think, through. Picture a quarry, follow the strata of the rock layer upon layer with a downward moving spiral. A downward movement rounded towards the center or from side to side, one hand pressed upon the other. Thistle, thimble, spiral inward up or down with wrists hanging down. Write in the sand from the wrists — the body moves in the opposite direction.	
Th	*Voiced* Mother, thither.	

Follow the movement of a plough throwing up the
furrows or the kneading of butter.
For words like this, that, these, and those.
A strong downward spiral movement with one hand,
the hand held almost at right angles to the wrist to
experience resistance.
A voiced Th can also dissolve upward:
"Thee without
Thou within."
Th can end in the S position.

The elements of earth and water are predominant in the English language, but the wind also blows over the waves, water and rock. Awareness of oneself, awareness of the world around. Form and transformation, tangible intangible, continuous movement.

The everchanging vowel sounds are as pebbles under rippling water; it is not possible to see their true shape and color until they are lifted out of the water. Then they become the primary vowels. The nature of the English vowel sound is to change and transform itself according to the neighboring consonants.

The essential character of English Eurythmy lies in the movement between the sounds, between words, between sentences. It lies in the music of the interval. The forms Dr. Steiner gave for the Shakespeare songs, for instance, bring out this musical quality in every detail.

The landscape, the weather, the elements are still very much part of the English language and should come to expression as much as the historical blending of northern and southern cultures.

About the Author

Molly von Heider was born in 1913 in Worcester, England, and after attending Waldorf Schools for the last three years of her school life, embarked upon a training in Eurythmy, a new art of movement inaugurated byDr. Rudolf Steiner. Further training in therapeutic Eurythmy and Education followed. She has taught for over 30 years, and her pupils have ranged from normal children to children with learning disabilities, factory workers, industrially injured people and trainee teachers.

Before and during the war Mrs. von Heider worked with Else Klink at the Eurythmeum, Stuttgart, until it, along with all other Rudolf Steiner institutions in Germany, was closed down. She spent the rest of the war years in a small village in Swabia, where her two daughters were born.

Mrs. von Heider has travelled extensively and has given Eurythmy and Education Courses in many parts of the world. She now teaches at Emerson College, an international centre for adult education based on the work of Rudolf Steiner.

Random Tips for Eurythmy Teachers

1. Never try to shout children down. Their lungs are stronger than yours. Get a child with a good loud voice to establish order and quiet.

2. Some children play up to attract attention; if you keep correcting them, it makes them worse. Be economical with corrections. Try to get their interest by humour and imagination, and always demand that exercises are done properly.

3. Class Eurythmy is NOT good for all children; one hyperactive child can wreck a class. It is better to do Eurythmy alone with such a child and arrange for him/her to be occupied elsewhere during Eurythmy lessons. The effect of many children running or clapping, can be too much for a hyperactive child. He or she gets over-excited, excarnated.

4. Never begin a lesson until all the children are clean and tidy and quiet. It doesn't matter how long it takes; it is worth it.

5. Do not keep a child in after school without informing the parents.

6. If the boys are being silly, pounce on the girls; the boys will stop and listen. Same approach if the girls are silly.

7. Be cheerful, hearty and strict. Speak normally, never in a 'holy' or sentimental voice. Children hate Eurythmy when they do it badly. The art is to renew the exercises in a joyful way until the children can do them well.

8. Put older children on the stage, they will then do their best and Eurythmy will have meaning for them.

9. Have a Eurythmy Festival every year in which each class shows the rest of the school and the parents what has been learned. For classes 1 and 2 it should be unrehearsed, like a lesson in a circle where the children imitate the teacher. Two afternoons would be needed, one for the Lower School and one for the Upper School.

10. If it is difficult to write on the blackboard (if it is greasy), let some of the children come up and breathe on it, preferably the noisy ones.

11. With the younger classes, do not explain. Talk as little as possible; the children learn by imitating, not by understanding intellectually.

12. If you are doing a story in the Eurythmy lesson, live totally in the story. If it takes you on a winding path through the forest, not only do you see the trees, ferns and mosses, you have to smell the pines and damp decaying leaves too.

13. Always have two helpers, one at the beginning and one at the end of the line. After the lesson, announce the helpers for next week and tell in a few words to what they can look forward.

14. Never forget birthdays. Let the birthday child choose his/her favourite exercise, poem or music. For

the younger children have a Eurythmy birthday game, such as "The Wild Beast", or the Arjuna exercise.

15. If you want to introduce something new to older pupils, never talk to them when they are standing; always let them sit down. Sometimes it is better to talk to them in the classroom, especially when working with geometry or answering questions such as: "why do we do Eurythmy; they don't do it in the grammar school?" If young people have questions, don't fob them off by saying, "because Eurythmy is good for you". (It is not good for them when they do it badly). Young people should be taken seriously. Often they have an intuitive understanding which they want to make conscious.

16. One way of dealing with this problem, which inevitably arises, is to let the children keep Eurythmy books from Class 4 or 5 on. This should be arranged with the Class Teacher. Also once a week they should have Eurythmy homework to draw the Eurythmy patterns and write the poems they have been learning in the Eurythmy lessons. In the Upper School tasks can be given, such as: writing a verse in hexameters; writing a story about the evolutionary sequence; naming and drawing an expanding tree and a contracting tree (willow, oak); finding spirals in nature and drawing one.

17. Never have a Class Teacher in a class to act as 'policeman' just to keep order. This will rob you of your own discipline BUT welcome any Class Teacher who will enjoy doing Eurythmy with the class. The children's enjoyment will be enhanced.

18. Take an interest in the children and their hobbies and school work other than Eurythmy. Go to watch them doing gym; cheer them when they are playing games; admire their woodwork and handwork; and look at their main lesson books, even if it is only once a term.

19. Never wear dull, drab clothes when teaching Eurythmy. Have big pockets for surprises such as crystals, starfish or snail shells.

20. Don't insist on keeping all the windows closed! It is not a Eurythmy training. Have a warm airy room. Children need fresh air.

21. Always work together with the Class Teacher. Let the Class Teacher introduce new subjects before you bring them in Eurythmy. Your working together with the Class Teacher gives the children a sense of security and deepens the main lesson work.

22. Avoid sarcasm; use humour instead.

Cross Reference Index

YS = COME UNTO THESE YELLOW SANDS

TH = AND THEN TAKE HANDS

Ballads

Deep asleep, deep asleep ....YS 167

I canna tell what has come o'er me ....YS 166

Sir Olaf he rideth west and east ....TH 48

The King was on his throne ....TH 49

Basic Forms and Indications

Alliterations

Barque, bravest in battle of billows and breeze ....YS 110

Behold there breaketh ....YS 174

Blow, bellow, blow ....TH 35

Erce, Erce, Erce, Mother of Earth ....TH 50

Forge me with Fire ....YS 109

In earliest times did Ymir live ....YS 108

I saw a sweet and simple sight ....YS 174

I sing of myself a song of sorrow ....TH 51

I war with the wind, with the waves I wrestle ....YS 105

My robe is silent when I rest on earth ....YS 105

Needful, Needful, masterful sword ....TH 37

O'er a mound on the morrow he merrily rides ....TH 51

On a May morning on the Malvern Hills ....YS 173

She was brighter of her blee, then was the bright soon ....YS 181

She was grisly and great and grim to behold ....YS 181

Swart, smirched smiths smattered with smoke ....YS 110

Appollonian Forms

He clasps the crag with crooked hands ....YS 103

The cock is crowing ....YS 145

When I conquer within me fear and wrath ....YS 164

Story

The Turnip ....YS 71

215

Concentration Exercises

(See diagram YS 98.)

Continuous Forms

I canna tell what has come o'er me

(See diagrams YS 167.)

Concentration and Expansion

Earth is dark and fear is lurking ....YS 85

I gather all my strength to fight ....YS 91

I'm so weak, and so are you ....YS 87

In the darkest night ....YS 32

I think I see an enemy ....YS 91

Sol revenit ....YS 190

The eternal light it shines in here ....YS 182

The leaves said: 'It's Spring' ....YS 53

The people that walked in darkness ....YS 183

We are robbers bold and burly ....YS 91

Welcome all wonders in one sight ....YS 182

When days are darkest the earth enshrines ....YS 91

When thou risest in the eastern horizon of heaven ....YS 129

While the earth remaineth ....YS 84

Crown Form

As I sat on a sunny bank, a sunny bank, a sunny bank ....YS 47

As up the wood I took my way ....YS 165

Up now, laggardly lasses ....YS 165

When Goodman winter comes again ....YS 96

Curve of Cassini

I was once young upon a day ....YS 187

On the earth I love to stand ....YS 46

The boughs do shake and the bells do ring ....YS 94

Young and alone along a long road ....YS 108

Elemental Forms

Christ, King of the Elements ....TH 45

Laudato si, mi signore ....YS 146

We go to seek the Winter King ....YS 75

Energy and Peace Dance

All this night shrill Chanticleer ....YS 146

King Arthur's walls are strong and steep ....TH 41

Evolutionary Sequence
(See diagrams YS 195)
He bears a burden in a sack (Lower School) .... YS 59

Harmonious Eight
Hail King! Hail King! .... TH 32
Joy and woe are woven fine .... TH 46
Now that the Winter's gone, the earth has lost .... YS 189
Shall I tell you who will come .... YS 49
Twist ye, twine ye! Even so .... TH 46

Inner and Outer Forces
In flaming fire we worship thee .... YS 128
The frost is here .... YS 130
The great sea has set me in motion .... YS 162

Maze
See diagram YS 193.)

Measures (Auftakt)
Merry measure
Merry are the bells and merry would they ring .... YS 187
O, I am as happy as a big sunflower .... YS 187
The whole bright world rejoices now .... YS 132
We've ploughed our field .... YS 95
Cosmic measure
Thy dawn, O Ra, opens the new horizon .... YS 191
The eye of the great God .... YS 191

Past, Present and Future
I am Yesterday, Today and Tomorrow .... TH 43
Look to this day .... TH 129

Question and Answer
Shall I tell you who will come? .... YS 49
What do we plant when we plant a tree? .... TH 31
What is the blossom that blooms in the snow? .... YS 130
Whenever the moon and the stars are set .... YS 35

Rotations and Inversions
Constellations come and climb the heavens and go .... YS 163
God bless the field - bless the furrow .... TH 38
The cock is crowing .... YS 145

Rhythms

Beat on the buckskins, beat on the drums .... YS 163
Bird of the wilderness .... TH 38
Blow wind, blow! Go mill, go! .... YS 94
Brave and true I will be .... YS 86
By the moon we sport and play .... TH 23
Dark brown is the river .... TH 27
Deep asleep, deep asleep .... YS 167
Earth! Thou mother of numberless children, the nurse and the mother ...... YS 144
Full merrily rings the millstone round .... TH 23
Greek rhythms (See diagram YS 140.)
Hail to Prometheus, the Titan, the helper of man and creator .... TH 42
Hie away! Hie away! .... YS 143
In May I go a-walking to hear the linnet sing .... YS 141
Kindle the fire flames .... YS 144
Many wonders there be but naught more wondrous than Man .... TH 42
Magic door .... YS 57
My father said .... TH 26
My mother said .... YS 58
Of wounds and sore defeat .... YS 143
Over hill, over dale .... YS 142
Over the mountain aloft ran a rush and a roll and a roaring .... YS 145
Pease pudding hot .... YS 58
Sound the flute! .... TH 33
Stepping over stepping stones, one, two, three .... YS 57
The Assyrian came down like the wolf on the fold .... TH 49
The boughs do shake and the bells do ring .... YS 94
There was a naughty boy .... YS 142
The silence was deep with a breath like sleep .... TH 39
The waters are flashing .... YS 141
To sea, to sea! The calm is o'er .... YS 186
Up on their brooms the witches stream .... YS 147
We are they who come faster than fate .... YS 143
We will go for a walk in our garden fair .... YS 58
When the Lord the mighty winged .... TH 32
Who is this who cometh as in conquest? .... YS 144
Winter creeps .... YS 97
Would that my father had taught me the craft of a keeper of sheep .... YS 145
You can't catch me! .... TH 25

Spirals

A little boy went into a barn .... YS 2-7
Behold a babe in Bethlehem .... YS 96
Behold the plant within the seed .... YS 164
Brown and furry .... TH 16
Day arises .... YS 162

Day had awakened all things that be .... TH 33
Down with the lamb .... YS 27
Earth is dark and fear is lurking .... YS 85
Five tiny fairies hiding in a flower .... YS 27
God is as small as I .... YS 184
Here we come .... YS 55
I have made a footprint, a sacred one .... TH 39
In the heart of a seed .... TH 16
I saw a little snail house .... TH 15
Little plant, little plant .... TH 16
Little snail, little snail .... TH 15
Minnie and Winnie .... YS 29
My house has an open door .... YS 83
Now that the Winter's gone, the earth has lost .... YS 189
Pit, pat, well-a-day! .... YS 27
Softly, softly in I creep .... YS 51
The eternal light it shines in here .... YS 182
The light of the sun gives strength to all things on earth .... YS 184
Said the wind to the moon, 'I will blow you out' .... TH 53
Waken sleeping butterfly .... YS 55
Welcome all wonders in one sight .... YS 182
Winter creeps .... YS 97
When thou risest in the eastern horizon of heaven .... YS 129

Straight Lines and Curves

Ave maria stella .... YS 182
Dark brown is the river .... TH 27
Four strong walls .... YS 59
God with all commanding might .... YS 96
Golden in the garden .... TH 34
Hark! The tiny cowslip bell .... TH 33
I'll seek you .... YS 201
Look up and behold .... YS 164
Pack, clouds, away, and welcome day .... YS 188
Spring is coming, Spring is coming .... TH 17
The year's at the Spring .... YS 131
We are the stars that sing .... YS 163

Thinking, Feeling and Willing Forms

My heart leaps up when I behold .... YS 188

Vowel Sounds

Ah! Ah! Ah! We shepherds see the star .... YS 48
I will prove alone .... TH 40
On the earth I love to stand .... YS 46

Pack, clouds, away, and welcome day .... YS 188

The sun says, 'I glow' .... YS 47

Verses for 'I' 'A' 'O' .... YS 35

We are the stars that sing .... YS 163

(See diagrams YS 194.)

Cultures and Nations

American Indian

Beat on the buckskins, beat on the drums .... YS 163

I have made a footprint, a sacred one .... TH 39

I will prove alone .... TH 40

The sun is a luminous shield .... YS 162

Thonah! Thonah! .... TH 40

We are the stars that sing .... YS 163

Ancient Indian

Nay, but as one layeth .... YS 128

Look to the day .... YS 129

Biblical

In eight parts God made Man .... YS 158

Old Tubal Cain was a man of might .... TH 30

The Assyrian came down like the wolf on the fold .... TH 49

The King was on his throne .... TH 49

The people that walked in darkness .... YS 183

This I learnt among men .... YS 95

When the Lord the mighty winged .... TH 32

While the earth remaineth .... YS 84

Celctic, Gaelic

Christ, King of the Elements .... TH 45

Hail King! Hail King! .... TH 32

I arise today .... TH 44

The eye of the great God .... YS 191

Legend

The Legend of Saint Bride .... TH 66

Plays

The Coming of Oisin .... TH 187

The Story of Fionn .... TH 167

Egyptian

Hail to thee, O Ra, O perfect and eternal one .... TH 143

I am Yesterday, Today, and Tomorrow .... TH 43

That which is below is like that which is above .... TH 43

Thy dawn, O Ra, opens the new horizon .... YS 191

When thou risest in the eastern horizon of heaven .... YS 129

Eskimo

Day arises .... YS 162

The great sea has set me in motion .... YS 162

The silence was deep with a breath like sleep (Antarctic) .... YS 39

Greek

Greek rhythms .... YS 140

Hail to Prometheus, the Titan, the helper of man and creator .... TH 42

Kindle the fire flames .... YS 144

Many wonders there be but naught more wondrous than Man .... TH 42

Over the mountain aloft ran a rush and a roll and a roaring .... YS 145

Who is this who cometh as in conquest? .... YS 144

Plays

Persephone .... YS 133

Theseus .... TH 135

Norse

Barque, bravest in battle of billows and breeze .... YS 110

Behold there breaketh .... YS 174

Blow, bellows, blow .... TH 35

I am the God Thor .... TH 34

I heard a voice that cried .... TH 36

In earliest times did Ymir live .... YS 108

I sing of myself a song of sorrow .... TH 51

I war with the wind, with the waves I wrestle .... YS 105

My robe is silent when I rest on earth .... YS 105

Needful, Needful, masterful sword .... TH 37

This I learnt among men .... YS 95

Wind 'tis called among menfolk .... YS 104

Young and alone on a long road .... YS 108

Play

Iduna and the Golden Apples .... YS 115

Persian

In flaming fire we worship thee .... YS 128

Scottish

Play

The Lord of Lorne .... YS 148

Elves and Fairies

All Hallows Eve ....YS 148

By summer enchanted ....YS 56

By the moon we sport and play ....TH 23

Five tiny fairies hiding in a flower ....YS 27

Full merrily rings the millstone round ....TH 23

I canna tell what has come ower me ....YS 166

Rip, rap, tick, tack ....YS 66

Walk along, skip along, dance along with me ....YS 57

You can't catch me! ....TH 25

Legend

The Ragweed ....YS 66

Plays

Midsummer Eve ....YS 196

The Elfin Cap ....TH 112

Farming

Blow wind, blow! Go mill, go; ....YS 94

Erce, Erce, Erce: Mother of Earth ....TH 50

For the dark earth that cradles the seed ....YS 90

Here stands a good apple tree ....YS 94

In Autumn Saint Michael with sword and with shield ....YS 92

Mother Earth ....YS 90

My maid Mary ....YS 95

Old Tubal Cain was a man of might ....TH 30

The boughs do shake and the bells do ring ....YS 94

The sun says: 'I glow' ....YS 47

Throughout the year ....TH 30

We've ploughed our field ....YS 95

Legend: Saint Michael and the Devil as Farmers ....TH 62

Saint Michael and the Scythe ....YS 113

Plays: For our Daily Bread we thank Thee, Father ....YS 92

Harvest Masque ....YS 114

Finger and Hand Games

TH pp 3-12; YS pp 24-26

House Building and Blessing

Beechwood fires are bright and clear ....TH 31

Blesse ye foure corners of thys House ....TH 32

Hail King! Hail King! ....TH 32

My house has an open door to the world so wide ....YS 83

Spirits of Sun, Earth and Air ....YS 95

What do we plant when we plant a tree? ....TH 31

With oak the old time ships were laid ....TH 32

Stories:Saint Michael's Mount ....TH 61

The Master Builder ....TH 77

Humourous Poems

Goblins came on mischief bent ....YS 168

I knew an old lady who swallowed a fly ....TH 52

No sun - no moon! ....TH 53

Out of his hole ....YS 170

Said the Wind to the Moon, 'I will blow you out' ....TH 53

The common cormorant or shag ....YS 169

There were three men a-finding ....YS 51

Man, Animals, Birds and Insects

Brown and furry ....TH 16

Bird of the wilderness ....TH 38

He clasps the crag with crooked hands ....YS 103

Larki, Larki, Larki Lee! ....TH 24

Low on his fours the Lion ....YS 112

Steadfast I'll stand in the world ....YS 111

The cat she walks on padded claws ....YS 112

Wee, sleekit, cow'rin tim'rous beastie ....TH 38

Legends

The Glowworm ....YS 70

The Nightingale ....YS 67

The Robin ....YS 68

The Spider ....YS 69

The Easter Hare ....YS 68

Repetitive Poems and Stories

A little tree stood in a wood ....TH 29

I know an old lady who swallowed a fly ....TH 52

Over the meadow in the sand and the sun ....TH 8

Then up and spake the stepmother ....TH 20

There was a tree upon a hill ....TH 18

There were three jolly musicians, musicians, musicians ....TH 22

The Queen she was a-weeping ....YS 17

This is the Key of the Kingdom ....TH 17

Plays

For our Daily Bread we thank Thee, Father ....YS 92
We are the good brown Earth ....YS 73

Stories

The Little White House at the Edge of the Wood ....TH 58
The Old Woman and her Pig ....TH 57
The Turnip ....YS 71

Riddles

We went to the wood and caught it ....TH 37
I am invisible ....YS 106
I war with the wind, with the waves I wrestle ....YS 105
My robe is silent when I rest on earth ....YS 105
Runs all day and never walks ....TH 37
Two brothers we are ....TH 37

Seasons and Festivals

Spring

From the hills flow the streamlets ....YS 54
Hark! The tiny cowslip bell ....TH 33
Here we come creepy-creep ....YS 55
Hie away! Hie away! ....YS 143
In May I go a-walking ....YS 141
In the heart of a seed ....TH 16
Mother Earth, mother Earth ....YS 90
Now that Winter's gone, the earth has lost ....YS 189
On a May morning on the Malvern Hills ....YS 173
Pack, clouds, away, and welcome day ....YS 188
Shee was brighter of her blee, than was the bright sonn ....YS 181
Sol revenit ....YS 190
Sound the flute! ....TH 33
Spring is coming, spring is coming ....TH 17
Spring, the sweet spring, is the year's pleasant King ....TH 33
The sun is gone down ....YS 52
The whole bright world rejoices now ....YS 132
The World itself keeps Easter Day ....YS 131
The year's at the spring ....YS 131
Waken sleeping butterfly ....YS 55
'Where are the snowdrops?' said the sun ....YS 3

Legends

The Cowslips ....YS 62
The Easter Hare ....YS 68

Play

Persephone ....YS 133

Summer

By summer enchanted ....YS 56
For flowers that bloom about our feet ....YS 2
The lightning and thunder ....YS 30
We each and everyone ....YS 70

Legend

The Glowworm ....YS 70

Plays

Faithful and Unfaithful ....TH 122
Midsummer Eve ....YS 196
The Elfin Cap ....TH 112

Autumn

All Hallow's Eve it is tonight ....YS 148
'Come little leaves', said the Wind one day ....TH 28
Earth is dark and fear is lurking ....YS 85
Golden in the garden ....TH 34
Here stands a good apple tree ....YS 94
I'm so weak and so are you ....YS 87
In Autumn Saint Michael with sword and with shield ....YS 92
Look up and behold ....YS 164
No sun - no moon! ....TH 53
O strong unconquered Knight of God ....YS 86
The boughs do shake and the bells do ring ....YS 94
Up on their brooms the witches stream ....YS 147
We've ploughed our field ....YS 95
When over the moon and the stars are set ....TH 35
When I conquer within me fear and wrath ....YS 164

Legends

Saint Michael and the Devil as Farmers ....TH 62
Saint Michael and the Dragon of Ireland ....YS 88
Saint Michael and the Hermit ....TH 64
Saint Michael and the Scythe ....YS 113
The Building of Saint Michael's Mount ....TH 61
Why the Soles of our Feet are not flat ....TH 63

Plays

All Hallowe'en ....TH 220
Harvest Masque ....YS 114
Michaelmas Play ....YS 79
Saint George and the Dragon ....TH 109
The Crooked Cross ....TH 229

Winter

Ah! Ah! Ah! We shepherds see the star . . . . YS 48

Ah! Dark is the sky . . . . YS 31

All this night shrill Chanticleer . . . . YS 146

As I sat on a sunny bank, a sunny bank, a sunny bank . . . . YS 47

As Joseph was a-walking . . . . TH 45

As up the wood I took my way . . . . YS 165

Ave maria stella . . . . YS 182

Behold a Babe in Bethlehem . . . . YS 96

Christ, King of the Elements . . . . TH 45

In the darkest night . . . . YS 32

I saw a sweet and simple sight . . . . YS 174

Lullaby, lullaby, Holy Child . . . . YS 32

Now all created things that be . . . . TH 95

0 little Lord we bring to thee . . . . TH 17

Shall I tell you who will come . . . . YS 49

She was grisly and great and grim to behold . . . . YS 181

The eternal light it shines in here . . . . YS 182

The frost is here . . . . YS 130

The people that walked in darkness . . . . YS 183

The stork she rose on Christmas Eve . . . . TH 46

Up now, laggardly lasses . . . . YS 165

Welcome all wonders in one night . . . . YS 182

When days are darkest the earth enshrines . . . . YS 91

When Goodman Winter comes again . . . . YS 96

Legends

The Christmas Rose . . . . TH 69

The Glowworm . . . . YS 70

The Holy Night . . . . TH 65

The Ladysmock and Marshmarigold . . . . YS 63

The Legend of Saint Bride . . . . TH 66

The Nightingale . . . . YS 67

The Poplar and the Holly . . . . YS 64

The Robin . . . . YS 68

The Snowdrops . . . . YS 63

Why the Spider has a Cross . . . . YS 69

To Great Astonishment . . . . TH 47

Plays

Shepherd's Play . . . . TH 101

Sun, Sun, Glorious One . . . . YS 72

We are the good brown Earth . . . . YS 73

We go to seek the Winter King . . . . YS 75

Zacharias Christmas Play . . . . TH 246

All Four Seasons

O Sun, so bright ....YS 46

The leaves said: 'It's Spring' ....YS 53

Winter creeps ....YS 97

Stones, Plants, Stars and Planets

Stones

An emerald is as green as grass ....TH 39

Plants

Behold the plant within the seed ....YS 164

Hark! The tiny cowslip bell ....TH 33

In the heart of a seed ....TH 16

Little plant, little plant ....TH 16

What is the blossom that blooms in the snow? ....YS 130

Legends

The Christmas Rose ....TH 69

The Convolvulus ....YS 65

The Cowslips ....YS 62

The Daisies ....YS 64

The Fir Tree ....TH 29

The Ladysmock and Marshmarigold ....YS 63

The Moss ....YS 65

The Ragweed ....YS 66

The Snowdrops ....YS 63

Stars and Planets

Constellations come and climb the heavens and go ....YS 163

Harken, hark! The hours careering ....YS 191

Sol revenit ....YS 190

Sun and moon and stars ....YS 32

The eye of the great God ....YS 191

The sun is a luminous shield ....YS 162

Up on their brooms the witches stream ....YS 147

We are the stars that sing ....YS 163